Refinancing Commercial Debt with SBA Mortgage Loans

How to Use SBA Mortgage Programs to Lower Payments and Improve Cash Flow

By Joseph G. Correa

Licensed Mortgage Broker, Finibi Mortgage

Copyright & Legal Notice

Published by Live Stronger Faster

The information provided in this book is for educational and informational purposes only and does not constitute financial, legal, tax, or investment advice. Although the author is a licensed mortgage professional, the content presented is general in nature and is not intended as personalized guidance for any specific individual, business, or financial situation.

The strategies, loan structures, and examples discussed in this book are illustrative and educational in nature. They are intended to demonstrate concepts related to SBA commercial mortgage financing, including SBA 7(a) and 504 loan programs, borrower qualification, debt service coverage

First Edition, 2026

Table of Contents

Introduction

Many entrepreneurs and property owners spend years focused on acquisition, growth, and operations, yet overlook one of the most impactful opportunities available to them: restructuring their existing debt to improve cash flow, reduce financial stress, and unlock new capital for expansion. This is where SBA mortgage refinancing becomes a game-changing tool. It is not simply about replacing one loan with another—it is about strategically repositioning your financial foundation to create long-term stability, flexibility, and growth potential. In this book, you will discover how refinancing commercial debt through SBA mortgage programs can transform your business, your property portfolio, and your financial trajectory.

Refinancing is often misunderstood. Many borrowers assume it is only for those in distress or those seeking lower interest rates. While lowering rates can certainly be a benefit, SBA mortgage refinancing goes far beyond that. It can be used to consolidate high-interest debt, extend repayment terms, stabilize variable-rate loans, access trapped equity, and improve monthly cash flow in ways that directly impact your ability to operate and grow your business. Whether you currently have conventional loans, private financing, seller financing, or even multiple layers of debt, SBA programs provide structured, government-backed solutions designed to create sustainable and affordable financing.

One of the most important concepts to understand is that cash flow is the lifeblood of any business. It determines your ability to hire, invest, expand, and survive during economic shifts. Even profitable businesses can struggle if their debt obligations are too high or poorly structured. This is where SBA refinancing shines. By extending loan terms—often up to 25 years for real estate—and offering competitive, stable interest rates, SBA mortgage programs can significantly reduce monthly payments. This reduction in debt service can immediately free up capital that can be reinvested into your business, used for operational stability, or allocated toward new opportunities.

Throughout this book, you will learn how SBA refinancing differs from traditional refinancing. Conventional lenders often focus strictly on risk metrics, credit scores, and rigid underwriting guidelines. In contrast, SBA programs are designed to support small businesses by providing more flexible qualification criteria, longer terms, and a broader understanding of business performance. This flexibility allows borrowers who may not qualify for traditional refinancing to still access powerful financing solutions that can reshape their financial future. Another critical advantage of SBA refinancing is the ability to consolidate multiple debts into a single, manageable loan. Many business owners accumulate various forms of financing over time—lines of credit, equipment loans, merchant cash advances, and short-term notes. While each of these may have served a purpose at one point, together they can create a heavy and inefficient debt burden. SBA refinancing allows you to combine these obligations into one structured loan with a predictable payment, often at a lower overall cost. This simplification not only improves cash flow but also makes financial management significantly easier.

You will also explore how SBA refinancing can be used strategically to reposition your business for growth. Imagine reducing your monthly debt obligations while simultaneously improving your balance sheet. This creates a stronger financial profile, which can make it easier to qualify for future financing, attract investors, or expand into new markets. Refinancing is not just about solving current problems—it is about setting the stage for future success.

In addition, this book will guide you through the specific SBA programs that can be used for refinancing, including the SBA 7(a) and SBA 504 loan programs. Each program has its own structure, benefits, and ideal use cases. The SBA 7(a) program offers flexibility and can be used for a wide range of refinancing scenarios, including consolidating business debt and restructuring existing obligations. The SBA 504 program, on the other hand, is designed for long-term, fixed-rate financing of owner-occupied commercial real estate and can be an excellent option for refinancing existing real estate loans. Understanding when and how to use each program is essential to maximizing your results.

A key component of successful refinancing is timing. Interest rates, property values, business performance, and market conditions all play a role in determining the best moment to refinance. Acting too early or too late can impact the benefits you receive. This book will help you identify the optimal timing for refinancing and show you how to evaluate your current financial situation to determine whether refinancing makes sense for you.

You will also learn how lenders evaluate refinancing applications. While SBA programs are more flexible than conventional loans, they still require thorough documentation and analysis. Lenders will examine your business financials, tax returns, debt structure, property value, and overall ability to repay the loan. By understanding these requirements in advance, you can position yourself for a smoother approval process and increase your chances of success.

Another powerful concept covered in this book is equity extraction. Many commercial property owners have built significant equity over time but are unable to access it without selling the property. SBA refinancing can allow you to tap into that equity in certain scenarios, providing additional capital that can be used for business expansion, improvements, or other strategic investments. This turns your existing assets into active tools for growth rather than passive holdings.

Risk management is another important theme. Poorly structured debt can expose your business to unnecessary risk, especially if you are dealing with variable interest rates or short-term maturities. SBA refinancing can help you stabilize your debt by converting it into long-term, fixed-rate financing. This predictability allows you to plan more effectively and reduces the uncertainty that can come with fluctuating payments.

As you move through this book, you will also gain insight into real-world scenarios and strategies that demonstrate how SBA refinancing can be applied in practical situations. From reducing high-interest debt to restructuring complex financing arrangements, these examples will help you see how the concepts discussed can be implemented in your own business.

Ultimately, the goal of this book is to shift your perspective on debt. Instead of viewing it as a burden, you will learn how to use it as a strategic tool. When structured correctly, debt can support growth, improve cash flow, and create opportunities that would otherwise be out of reach. SBA mortgage refinancing is one of the most effective ways to achieve this, providing a pathway to financial efficiency and long-term success.

By the time you finish this book, you will have a clear understanding of how SBA refinancing works, when to use it, and how to structure it to your advantage. You will be equipped with the knowledge and strategies needed to evaluate your current debt, identify opportunities for improvement, and take action with confidence. Whether you are looking to lower your payments, consolidate debt, access equity, or position your business for growth, SBA mortgage refinancing offers a powerful solution—and this book will show you exactly how to use it.

Chapter 1

Understanding SBA Commercial Mortgage Loan Refinancing Fundamentals

Refinancing commercial debt is one of the most powerful financial strategies available to business owners, yet it is often misunderstood or underutilized. At its core, refinancing means replacing an existing loan with a new one, typically with better terms that improve your financial position. However, when it comes to SBA commercial mortgage loans, refinancing becomes much more than just swapping one loan for another. It becomes a strategic move that can reshape your cash flow, strengthen your balance sheet, and position your business for long-term success. In this chapter, you will gain a deep understanding of how SBA refinancing works, why it is different from conventional refinancing, and how it can be used to transform your commercial real estate and business financing.

To begin, it is important to understand why businesses refinance in the first place. Over time, many business owners accumulate debt under different circumstances. You may have taken out a loan when interest rates were higher, when your credit profile was weaker, or when your business was in an earlier stage of development. As your business grows and your financial position improves, the original loan may no longer be the most efficient option. The terms may be too restrictive, the payments too high, or the structure too inflexible. Refinancing allows you to revisit those terms and replace them with a loan that better reflects your current situation.

SBA refinancing stands apart from conventional refinancing because it is backed by government-supported programs designed specifically to help small businesses succeed. Programs such as the SBA 7(a) and SBA 504 loans provide lenders with a level of security that allows them to offer more favorable terms to borrowers. This includes longer repayment periods, lower down payment requirements in some cases, and more flexible underwriting criteria. For borrowers, this translates into a unique opportunity to restructure debt in a way that is often not possible through traditional financing.

One of the most immediate and impactful benefits of refinancing through an SBA mortgage loan is the potential to reduce your monthly payments. This is typically achieved by extending the loan term. For example, if you currently have a commercial loan with a remaining term of 10 years, refinancing into an SBA loan with a 25-year term can significantly lower your monthly obligation. While this may increase the total interest paid over time, the improvement in monthly cash flow can be a game changer for your business. Lower payments mean more flexibility, more stability, and more opportunities to reinvest in growth.

Another key benefit is the ability to secure a more favorable interest rate. Interest rates fluctuate over time based on market conditions, and if you originally secured your loan during a period of higher rates, refinancing can allow you to take advantage of lower rates. Additionally, SBA loans often offer competitive rates due to the government guarantee provided to lenders. This can result in meaningful savings over the life of the loan, especially when combined with extended terms.

Debt consolidation is another major advantage of SBA refinancing. Many businesses operate with multiple forms of debt, including lines of credit, equipment financing, and short-term loans. Managing these obligations can be complex and costly, particularly if they carry high interest rates. SBA refinancing allows you to combine these debts into a single loan with one payment, one interest rate, and one set of terms. This simplification not only reduces administrative burden but can also lower your overall cost of capital.

It is also important to understand the types of debt that can be refinanced using SBA programs. Generally, eligible debt includes existing commercial mortgages, business loans, and other obligations that were used for business purposes. The key requirement is that the refinancing must provide a clear benefit to the borrower, such as improved cash flow or more favorable terms. Lenders will evaluate the existing debt and determine whether refinancing meets SBA guidelines, ensuring that the transaction supports the long-term viability of the business.

Another critical concept is the difference between refinancing for rate-and-term purposes and refinancing for cash-out purposes. Rate-and-term refinancing focuses on improving the terms of the existing loan, such as lowering the interest rate or extending the repayment period. Cash-out refinancing, on the other hand, allows you to access the equity in your property or business assets and convert it into usable capital. This can be used for a variety of purposes, including expansion, renovations, or working capital. However, cash-out refinancing may be subject to additional requirements and limitations, depending on the SBA program and the specifics of the transaction.

The role of collateral is also an important factor in SBA refinancing. In most cases, the property being refinanced will serve as the primary collateral for the loan. Lenders will require an appraisal to determine its current market value and ensure that it supports the loan amount. In some cases, additional collateral may be required, particularly if the loan includes cash-out or if the borrower's financial profile presents additional risk. Understanding how collateral is evaluated can help you prepare for the refinancing process and set realistic expectations.

Creditworthiness and business performance are also key components of the refinancing process. While SBA programs are more flexible than conventional loans, lenders still need to ensure that the borrower has the ability to repay the loan. This includes reviewing financial statements, tax returns, credit history, and other relevant documentation. Strong financial performance and a solid repayment history can significantly improve your chances of approval and help you secure better terms.

Timing is another crucial element of successful refinancing. Market conditions, interest rates, and your business performance all play a role in determining the right time to refinance. For example, refinancing during a period of declining interest rates can maximize your savings, while refinancing after a period of strong business performance can improve your eligibility and terms. Understanding these factors allows you to make more informed decisions and take advantage of opportunities as they arise. Finally, it is important to approach refinancing with a strategic mindset. This is not just a transactional process—it is an opportunity to align your financing with your long-term goals. Whether you are looking to improve cash flow, reduce risk, or position your business for expansion, SBA refinancing provides a powerful set of tools to help you achieve those objectives. By understanding the fundamentals outlined in this chapter, you will be better equipped to evaluate your options, structure your refinancing strategy, and move forward with confidence.

Real-Life Math Example: SBA Commercial Mortgage Loan Refinancing Scenario

Imagine a business owner named Carlos who owns a small manufacturing company and an owner-occupied commercial property. Ten years ago, Carlos purchased the property for $1,200,000 and financed it with a conventional commercial mortgage. The original loan amount was $900,000, with an interest rate of 7.5% and a 20-year amortization schedule. His monthly payment was approximately $7,252. Over the past ten years, Carlos has made consistent payments and has reduced the loan balance to $650,000. However, his business has grown significantly, and he now finds that his current loan structure is limiting his ability to expand.

Carlos begins exploring SBA refinancing options and discovers that he may be eligible for an SBA 504 refinance. The current market value of his property has increased to $1,500,000, giving him substantial equity. He works with a lender to structure a new SBA loan that will refinance his existing $650,000 balance and provide additional cash-out for business expansion. The total new loan amount is structured at $900,000, which includes paying off the existing loan and accessing $250,000 in equity.

The new SBA loan is structured with a blended interest rate of 6% and a 25-year term. This significantly changes Carlos's financial picture. His new monthly payment on the $900,000 loan is approximately $5,800. Even though his loan amount has increased, his monthly payment has decreased by over $1,400 compared to his previous payment of $7,252. This immediate improvement in cash flow provides Carlos with additional financial flexibility.

Now let's break down the numbers in more detail. Under his original loan, Carlos was paying $7,252 per month for a remaining balance of $650,000 with about 10 years left on the term. Over those 10 years, he would have paid approximately $870,240 in total payments, including both principal and interest. With the new SBA loan, Carlos will pay $5,800 per month over 25 years, resulting in total payments of

$1,740,000. While this is a higher total due to the extended term, the key benefit lies in the reduced monthly obligation and the additional capital he receives. The $250,000 cash-out allows Carlos to invest in new equipment and expand his operations. This expansion is expected to increase his monthly revenue by $8,000. When combined with his reduced loan payment, Carlos's net monthly cash flow improves significantly. Previously, after accounting for his loan payment, his available cash flow was limited. Now, with an additional $8,000 in revenue and a $1,400 reduction in debt payments, his monthly financial position improves by $9,400.

This example highlights the power of SBA refinancing. By restructuring his debt, Carlos not only reduces his monthly payment but also unlocks capital that enables growth. The increased revenue from his expansion more than offsets the additional interest paid over the life of the loan. In this way, refinancing becomes an investment in the future of the business rather than simply a financial adjustment.

Additionally, Carlos benefits from the stability of a long-term loan with a predictable payment. This allows him to plan more effectively, manage his cash flow with confidence, and focus on growing his business without the pressure of high monthly debt obligations. Over time, as his business continues to grow, the relative impact of his loan payment decreases, further strengthening his financial position.

This real-life scenario demonstrates how SBA commercial mortgage refinancing can be used strategically to improve cash flow, access equity, and support business expansion. By understanding the numbers and evaluating both the short-term and long-term impacts, business owners can make informed decisions that align with their goals and maximize their financial potential.

Chapter 2

SBA 7(a) vs. SBA 504 Refinancing Strategies — Choosing the Right Loan for Maximum Impact

When it comes to refinancing commercial debt using SBA mortgage programs, one of the most important decisions you will make is choosing between the SBA 7(a) loan and the SBA 504 loan. Both programs are powerful, both are backed by the Small Business Administration, and both can dramatically improve your financial situation—but they are designed for different purposes, structured differently, and deliver different strategic advantages depending on your goals. Understanding how each program works and when to use one over the other is essential if you want to maximize the benefits of refinancing and position your business for long-term success.

The SBA 7(a) loan program is often considered the most flexible SBA financing option available. It can be used for a wide range of purposes, including refinancing existing business debt, consolidating multiple loans, accessing working capital, and even funding new business opportunities. This flexibility makes it an ideal choice for borrowers who have complex financial situations or multiple types of debt that need to be restructured into a single, manageable loan. One of the key advantages of the 7(a) program is that it allows you to refinance not only real estate debt but also other business obligations, such as lines of credit, equipment loans, and high-interest short-term financing.

In contrast, the SBA 504 loan program is specifically designed for long-term financing of owner-occupied commercial real estate and large equipment purchases. It is less flexible than the 7(a) program in terms of allowable uses, but it offers significant advantages in terms of stability and cost. The 504 program typically involves a two-part loan structure: one portion provided by a bank or lender and another portion provided by a Certified Development Company (CDC), which is backed by the SBA. This structure allows for long-term, fixed-rate financing, often at very competitive interest rates, making it particularly attractive for borrowers who want predictable payments and protection against rising interest rates.

One of the first factors to consider when choosing between these two programs is the type of debt you are refinancing. If your goal is to refinance a mix of real estate debt and other business obligations, the SBA 7(a) loan is usually the better option. Its flexibility allows you to consolidate multiple debts into one loan, simplifying your financial structure and potentially reducing your overall cost of capital. On the other hand, if you are primarily refinancing an existing commercial mortgage on an owner-occupied property, the SBA 504 loan may offer better long-term terms, particularly if you value fixed-rate stability.

Another important consideration is interest rate structure. SBA 7(a) loans often have variable interest rates, which means your rate can change over time based on market conditions. While these rates can be competitive, they introduce a level of uncertainty that may not be ideal for all borrowers. In contrast, SBA 504 loans typically offer fixed interest rates on the CDC portion of the loan, providing long-term predictability. For business owners who prioritize stability and want to lock in their financing costs, this can be a major advantage.

Loan term is another key difference between the two programs. Both SBA 7(a) and SBA 504 loans can offer long repayment periods—up to 25 years for real estate—but the structure and implications of those terms can vary. With a 7(a) loan, the flexibility of use is balanced by potentially higher overall costs due to variable rates. With a 504 loan, the longer term combined with fixed rates can result in more predictable and often lower effective costs over time, especially in stable or rising interest rate environments.

Prepayment penalties and restrictions also play a role in the decision-making process. SBA 504 loans often come with specific prepayment penalties, particularly in the early years of the loan, due to the bond-like structure of the CDC portion. This means that if you plan to refinance again or sell the property within a short timeframe, the 504 loan may not be the most flexible option. SBA 7(a) loans may also include prepayment penalties in certain situations, but they are generally more flexible, making them better suited for borrowers who anticipate future changes.

Cash-out refinancing is another area where these programs differ significantly. SBA 7(a) loans are generally more accommodating when it comes to accessing equity for working capital, expansion, or other business needs. This makes them ideal for borrowers who want to use refinancing as a way to fuel growth. SBA 504 loans can also allow for cash-out refinancing in certain cases, but the rules are more restrictive, and the primary focus remains on real estate financing.

Another critical factor is eligibility and qualification. While both programs are designed to support small businesses, they have different underwriting considerations. SBA 7(a) loans tend to be more flexible in terms of credit and financial requirements, making them accessible to a broader range of borrowers. SBA 504 loans, while still flexible compared to conventional financing, may require stronger financials and a clear alignment with program guidelines, particularly regarding property use and occupancy.

Strategically, the choice between SBA 7(a) and SBA 504 refinancing should align with your long-term business goals. If your primary objective is flexibility, debt consolidation, and access to capital, the 7(a) program is often the better choice. If your goal is to secure long-term, stable financing for a commercial property with predictable payments, the 504 program may be the superior option. In some cases, business owners may even use both programs at different stages of their growth, leveraging the strengths of each to achieve specific objectives.

It is also important to consider how each option impacts your overall financial strategy. Refinancing is not just about improving your current situation—it is about positioning your business for future opportunities. The right loan structure can enhance your ability to qualify for additional financing, improve your financial ratios, and create a more stable foundation for growth. By carefully evaluating the features and benefits of each SBA program, you can make a decision that supports both your immediate needs and your long-term vision.

Ultimately, choosing between SBA 7(a) and SBA 504 refinancing is about understanding your priorities and aligning them with the strengths of each program. There is no one-size-fits-all solution, and the best choice will depend on your unique circumstances. By mastering the concepts in this chapter, you will be equipped to evaluate your options, structure your refinancing strategy, and make informed decisions that maximize your financial potential.

Real-Life Math Example: Comparing SBA 7(a) vs. SBA 504 Refinancing Outcomes

Consider a business owner named Elena who owns a medical office building valued at $2,000,000. She currently has an existing commercial mortgage with a remaining balance of $1,200,000 at an interest rate of 7.25%, with 15 years remaining. Her monthly payment is approximately $10,900. In addition to this mortgage, she also has $200,000 in business debt from equipment loans and lines of credit with an average interest rate of 10%, resulting in monthly payments of $4,300. Her total monthly debt obligation is $15,200.

Elena is exploring refinancing options to reduce her monthly payments and improve her cash flow. She is considering two options: an SBA 7(a) loan and an SBA 504 loan. Let's analyze both scenarios.

In the SBA 7(a) scenario, Elena refinances her $1,200,000 mortgage and consolidates her $200,000 in additional business debt into a single loan of $1,400,000. The new loan has an interest rate of 6.75% and a 25-year term. Her new monthly payment is approximately $9,700. Compared to her previous total monthly obligation of $15,200, she reduces her payments by $5,500 per month. This immediate improvement in cash flow provides her with significant financial flexibility.

Over the life of the 25-year loan, Elena will pay approximately $2,910,000 in total payments, including principal and interest. While this is a substantial amount, it reflects the extended term and consolidated debt. The key advantage is the improved monthly cash flow and simplified financial structure, which allows her to focus on growing her practice.

In the SBA 504 scenario, Elena refinances only her real estate loan of $1,200,000. The loan is structured with 50% from a bank and 40% from a CDC, with the remaining 10% as equity. The blended interest rate is 6.25%, and the term is 25 years. Her new monthly payment on the real estate loan is approximately $7,900. However, her $200,000 in additional business debt remains separate, with monthly payments of $4,300. Her total monthly obligation becomes $12,200.

Compared to her original $15,200 monthly payment, she

reduces her payments by $3,000 per month. While this is less than the savings achieved with the 7(a) loan, she benefits from a lower interest rate on the real estate portion and greater long-term stability due to the fixed-rate structure of the 504 loan.

Now let's compare the outcomes. In the 7(a) scenario, Elena saves $5,500 per month and consolidates all her debt into one loan, but she takes on a slightly higher interest rate and variable rate exposure. In the 504 scenario, she saves $3,000 per month, maintains separate debts, but benefits from a lower fixed rate and long-term stability.

If Elena uses the additional cash flow from the 7(a) loan to invest in her business and generate an additional $7,000 per month in revenue, her net improvement becomes $12,500 per month. Over time, this can significantly outweigh the higher total interest paid. On the other hand, if she prefers stability and lower long-term costs, the 504 loan provides a more predictable financial structure.

This example illustrates how the choice between SBA 7(a) and SBA 504 refinancing is not just about numbers–it is about strategy. The best option depends on how the loan aligns with your goals, risk tolerance, and growth plans. By understanding the math and the strategic implications, you can make a decision that maximizes both your immediate benefits and your long-term success.

Chapter 3

Qualifying for SBA Commercial Mortgage Loan Refinancing – Requirements, Documentation, and Approval Strategy

Qualifying for SBA commercial mortgage loan refinancing is both an art and a science. While SBA programs are designed to be more flexible than conventional financing, they still require a structured and well-documented approach to ensure that the borrower meets the standards necessary for approval. Understanding how lenders evaluate your application, what documentation is required, and how to strategically position yourself as a strong borrower can dramatically increase your chances of success. In this chapter, you will learn exactly how the qualification process works, what lenders are looking for, and how to prepare your business and financial profile to secure approval with the best possible terms.

The first and most important concept to understand is that SBA lenders are focused on risk mitigation. Even though the loans are partially guaranteed by the government, lenders are still responsible for ensuring that the borrower has the ability to repay the loan. This means that every aspect of your financial profile will be analyzed, including your credit history, business performance, cash flow, debt structure, and collateral. The goal is to demonstrate that your business is stable, profitable, and capable of sustaining the new loan over the long term.

One of the primary factors in SBA refinancing approval is cash flow. Lenders will evaluate your Debt Service Coverage Ratio (DSCR), which measures your ability to cover your loan payments with your business income. Typically, lenders look for a DSCR of at least 1.25, meaning your business generates 25% more income than is required to cover your debt obligations. A higher DSCR indicates a stronger financial position and can improve your chances of approval as well as the terms offered. If your DSCR is currently below the desired threshold, restructuring your finances before applying can make a significant difference.

Another critical component is your credit profile. Both personal and business credit scores are taken into account during the underwriting process. While SBA programs are more forgiving than traditional loans, a strong credit history demonstrates reliability and reduces perceived risk. Lenders will look at your payment history, outstanding obligations, and any negative events such as late payments, collections, or bankruptcies. Improving your credit profile before applying—by paying down balances, resolving disputes, and maintaining consistent payment behavior—can enhance your approval prospects.

Collateral plays a major role in SBA refinancing as well. In most cases, the commercial property being refinanced will serve as the primary collateral for the loan. Lenders will require a professional appraisal to determine its current market value and ensure that it supports the loan amount. If the loan includes additional funds, such as cash-out refinancing, the collateral requirements may increase. In some situations, lenders may also require additional collateral, such as other business assets or personal guarantees, to strengthen the application.

Documentation is another key element of the qualification process. SBA loans require a comprehensive set of documents that provide a complete picture of your financial situation. This typically includes business and personal tax returns for the past two to three years, profit and loss statements, balance sheets, bank statements, and a detailed list of existing debts. You may also need to provide a business plan or a narrative explaining how the refinancing will benefit your business. Being organized and thorough with your documentation not only speeds up the process but also demonstrates professionalism and preparedness.

One of the unique aspects of SBA refinancing is the requirement that the transaction must provide a clear benefit to the borrower. This could include reducing monthly payments, improving cash flow, stabilizing interest rates, or consolidating debt. Lenders will analyze your current loan terms and compare them to the proposed refinancing terms to ensure that the new loan offers a meaningful advantage. This requirement ensures that SBA refinancing is used as a tool for improvement rather than simply replacing one obligation with another.

Another important factor is business history and stability. Lenders typically prefer businesses that have been operating for at least two years, as this provides a track record of performance. However, newer businesses may still qualify if they demonstrate strong financials and management experience. Consistency in revenue, profitability, and operations can significantly strengthen your application. Sudden fluctuations or inconsistencies may require additional explanation and documentation.

The structure of your existing debt also plays a role in the approval process. Lenders will evaluate the terms, interest rates, and repayment schedules of your current obligations to determine how refinancing will impact your overall financial position. High-interest or short-term debt is often viewed as a strong candidate for refinancing, as replacing it with a long-term SBA loan can provide immediate benefits. Understanding how your current debt is perceived by lenders can help you position your application more effectively.

Timing is another critical consideration. Applying for refinancing during a period of strong financial performance can improve your chances of approval and help you secure better terms. Conversely, applying during a downturn may make the process more challenging. Monitoring your financial metrics and market conditions allows you to choose the optimal time to apply, maximizing the benefits of refinancing.

Preparation is key to a successful application. Before approaching a lender, it is important to review your financials, identify any potential weaknesses, and address them proactively. This may involve reducing outstanding debt, improving cash flow, or organizing your documentation. Working with experienced professionals, such as accountants or financial advisors, can also provide valuable insights and help you present a stronger application.

Finally, it is important to approach the qualification process with a strategic mindset. This is not just about getting approved—it is about securing the right loan with the best possible terms. By understanding what lenders are looking for and aligning your application with those criteria, you can position yourself as a low-risk, high-quality borrower. This not only increases your chances of approval but also enhances your ability to negotiate favorable terms.

By mastering the concepts in this chapter, you will be equipped to navigate the SBA refinancing qualification process with confidence. You will understand how lenders evaluate your application, what steps you can take to improve your profile, and how to position your business for success. With the right preparation and strategy, SBA refinancing can become a powerful tool for improving your financial position and achieving your long-term goals.

Real-Life Math Example: Qualifying and Structuring an SBA Refinancing Approval

Consider a business owner named Marcus who owns a logistics company and an owner-occupied warehouse valued at $1,800,000. Marcus currently has a commercial mortgage with a remaining balance of $1,100,000 at an interest rate of 7.75%, with 12 years remaining. His monthly payment is approximately $11,200. In addition, he has $150,000 in business debt from equipment loans with monthly payments totaling $3,200. His total monthly debt obligation is $14,400.

Marcus's business generates an average net operating income of $18,000 per month. To calculate his DSCR, we divide his income by his total debt obligations. His current DSCR is 1.25 ($18,000 ÷ $14,400), which meets the minimum requirement for many SBA lenders but leaves little margin for error. Marcus wants to improve his cash flow and strengthen his financial position by refinancing his debt.

Marcus applies for an SBA 7(a) loan to refinance both his mortgage and his equipment debt into a single loan. The new loan amount is $1,250,000, with an interest rate of 6.75% and a 25-year term. His new monthly payment is approximately $8,600. This reduces his monthly debt obligation by $5,800 compared to his previous $14,400.

Now let's analyze the impact on his DSCR. With the new loan, his monthly income remains $18,000, but his debt obligation drops to $8,600. His new DSCR becomes approximately 2.09 ($18,000 ÷ $8,600). This represents a significant improvement in his financial stability and makes him a much stronger borrower in the eyes of lenders.

From a lender's perspective, this improvement in DSCR demonstrates that Marcus has a strong ability to repay the loan, reducing the overall risk of the transaction. This can lead to better loan terms, including lower interest rates and more favorable conditions. Additionally, the consolidation of his debt simplifies his financial structure, making it easier to manage and monitor. Now consider the long-term financial impact. Under his original loans, Marcus would have paid approximately $1,612,800 over the remaining term of his mortgage and equipment loans combined. With the new SBA loan, his total payments over 25 years will be approximately $2,580,000. While this represents a higher total due to the extended term, the key benefit lies in the improved monthly cash flow and financial stability.

Marcus uses the $5,800 in monthly savings to invest in expanding his logistics operations. This investment increases his monthly revenue by $7,500, raising his total monthly income to $25,500. With his new debt obligation of $8,600, his updated DSCR becomes approximately 2.97 ($25,500 ÷ $8,600). This positions him for future growth and additional financing opportunities.

This example illustrates how understanding and improving key financial metrics can play a critical role in qualifying for SBA refinancing. By restructuring his debt, Marcus not only improves his cash flow but also strengthens his overall financial profile, creating new opportunities for growth and success.

Chapter 4

Structuring the SBA Refinancing Deal – Terms, Leverage, and Cash Flow Optimization

Structuring an SBA commercial mortgage refinancing deal is where strategy meets execution. While qualifying for the loan is critical, the way the loan is structured ultimately determines how much benefit you receive from the transaction. A well-structured deal can dramatically improve cash flow, reduce risk, and create opportunities for future growth. On the other hand, a poorly structured deal—even if approved—can limit flexibility and reduce long-term financial efficiency. In this chapter, you will learn how to design your SBA refinancing structure intentionally, focusing on loan terms, leverage, interest rates, amortization, and how each component impacts your business.

The foundation of any refinancing structure begins with understanding loan terms. SBA loans offer extended amortization periods—typically up to 25 years for real estate—which is one of the most powerful tools available for improving cash flow. The longer the term, the lower the monthly payment, as the principal is spread over a greater number of years. However, this comes with a trade-off: longer terms generally result in more total interest paid over time. The key is to determine whether the monthly savings outweigh the long-term cost, especially when those savings can be reinvested into your business to generate higher returns.

Interest rate structure is another critical element. SBA 7(a) loans typically have variable interest rates tied to benchmarks such as the prime rate, while SBA 504 loans often include fixed-rate components. Choosing between variable and fixed rates is not just a financial decision—it is a risk management decision. Variable rates may offer lower initial costs but can increase over time, while fixed rates provide stability and predictability. When structuring your deal, you must consider your tolerance for risk, your expectations for future interest rate movements, and how rate changes could impact your cash flow.

Leverage is another powerful factor in SBA refinancing. Leverage refers to the amount of debt used relative to the value of the property or asset. SBA programs allow for relatively high leverage compared to conventional loans, often up to 90% loan-to-value in certain scenarios. This means you can refinance a significant portion of your property's value while retaining ownership. High leverage can be advantageous because it allows you to preserve capital and potentially access equity without selling the property. However, it also increases your debt obligations, so it must be balanced carefully with your cash flow capacity.

Cash-out refinancing is one of the most strategic uses of SBA loan structuring. If your property has appreciated in value, you may be able to access a portion of that equity and convert it into usable capital. This capital can then be reinvested into your business, used for renovations, or deployed into new opportunities. The key to successful cash-out structuring is ensuring that the additional debt does not negatively impact your financial stability. The goal is to use the borrowed funds in a way that generates returns greater than the cost of the loan.

Amortization structure also plays a significant role in how your loan performs over time. SBA loans are typically fully amortizing, meaning each payment includes both principal and interest, and the loan is paid off completely by the end of the term. This is different from some conventional commercial loans that may include balloon payments. A fully amortizing loan eliminates the risk of a large lump-sum payment at the end of the term, providing greater long-term stability. However, understanding how your payments are allocated between principal and interest can help you make more informed decisions about prepayments and long-term planning.

Another important consideration is prepayment strategy. While SBA loans may include prepayment penalties in certain cases, especially in the early years, planning your repayment strategy can still provide significant benefits. Making additional principal payments when possible can reduce the total interest paid over the life of the loan and shorten the effective loan term. Structuring your deal with flexibility in mind allows you to take advantage of these opportunities when your cash flow improves.

Debt consolidation is often a central component of SBA refinancing. By combining multiple debts into a single loan, you can simplify your financial structure and potentially reduce your overall cost of capital. However, it is important to analyze the terms of each existing debt and ensure that consolidation provides a net benefit. In some cases, certain debts may have favorable terms that should be maintained separately. A strategic approach to consolidation ensures that you maximize efficiency without sacrificing advantageous conditions.

The impact of refinancing on your financial ratios is another critical factor. Metrics such as DSCR, loan-to-value ratio, and overall leverage will influence not only your current loan approval but also your ability to secure future financing. Structuring your loan in a way that strengthens these metrics can position your business for additional growth opportunities. For example, lowering your monthly payments can improve your DSCR, making you a more attractive borrower for future loans.

It is also important to consider how your refinancing structure aligns with your long-term business goals. If your objective is to expand, you may prioritize cash-out and lower monthly payments to free up capital. If your goal is stability, you may focus on fixed rates and predictable terms. Every decision in the structuring process should be guided by your broader strategy, ensuring that your financing supports your vision rather than constraining it.

Risk management is another essential aspect of structuring your deal. This includes evaluating how changes in interest rates, market conditions, or business performance could impact your ability to repay the loan. By stress-testing your financial projections and considering different scenarios, you can design a loan structure that remains sustainable under various conditions. This proactive approach reduces uncertainty and provides greater confidence in your financial planning.

Ultimately, structuring an SBA refinancing deal is about creating a balance between cost, flexibility, and opportunity. It requires a deep understanding of how each component of the loan interacts with your business and your financial goals. By mastering these concepts, you can transform refinancing from a simple transaction into a powerful strategic tool that drives growth, stability, and long-term success.

Real-Life Math Example: Structuring an SBA Refinancing Deal for Maximum Cash Flow

Consider a business owner named Sophia who owns a mixed-use commercial property valued at $2,500,000. She currently has an existing loan balance of $1,500,000 at an interest rate of 8%, with 15 years remaining. Her monthly payment is approximately $14,300. In addition, she has $250,000 in high-interest business debt with monthly payments totaling $6,000. Her total monthly debt obligation is $20,300.

Sophia is exploring SBA refinancing options to improve her cash flow and access capital for expansion. She works with a lender to structure an SBA 7(a) loan that will refinance her existing mortgage and consolidate her business debt. The total new loan amount is $1,900,000, which includes paying off her existing obligations and providing $150,000 in additional cash-out.

The new loan has an interest rate of 6.75% and a 25-year term. Her new monthly payment is approximately $13,100. Compared to her previous total monthly obligation of $20,300, she reduces her payments by $7,200 per month. This immediate improvement in cash flow provides significant financial flexibility. Now let's analyze the leverage. With a property value of $2,500,000 and a loan amount of $1,900,000, her loan-to-value ratio is 76%. This is within acceptable SBA guidelines and allows her to access equity while maintaining a reasonable level of leverage. The $150,000 cash-out provides additional capital that she uses to renovate part of the property, increasing rental income.

The renovations increase her monthly rental income by $5,500. When combined with her $7,200 reduction in debt payments, her total monthly financial improvement is $12,700. This significantly enhances her cash flow and strengthens her financial position.

Over the life of the loan, Sophia will pay approximately $3,930,000 in total payments. While this is higher than her original loan due to the extended term and increased loan amount, the key benefit lies in the improved monthly cash flow and the additional income generated from her investment. The returns from her renovations exceed the cost of the additional debt, making the refinancing a strategic success.

Additionally, her DSCR improves significantly. Before refinancing, her income was approximately $25,000 per month, with debt obligations of $20,300, resulting in a DSCR of 1.23. After refinancing, her income increases to $30,500, and her debt obligations decrease to $13,100, resulting in a DSCR of 2.33. This makes her a much stronger borrower and positions her for future financing opportunities.

This example demonstrates how thoughtful structuring of an SBA refinancing deal can transform a business's financial landscape. By optimizing loan terms, leveraging equity, and aligning the structure with her goals, Sophia is able to improve her cash flow, increase her income, and create new opportunities for growth.

Chapter 5

Cash-Out Refinancing Strategies – Turning Equity into Growth Capital

Cash-out refinancing is one of the most powerful strategies available within SBA commercial mortgage lending, yet it is also one of the most misunderstood. Many business owners view their commercial property as a static asset—something that holds value but does not actively contribute to growth unless sold. In reality, that property can be transformed into a dynamic financial tool. Through SBA cash-out refinancing, you can unlock the equity you have built over time and convert it into capital that can be reinvested into your business, used to acquire additional assets, or deployed to increase profitability. In this chapter, you will learn how to strategically use cash-out refinancing, how to evaluate whether it makes sense, and how to ensure that the capital you extract creates a return that exceeds the cost of borrowing.

To begin, it is important to understand what equity represents. Equity is the difference between the current market value of your property and the outstanding balance of your loan. As your property appreciates in value and as you pay down your loan over time, your equity grows. This equity is often referred to as "trapped capital" because it exists on paper but is not readily accessible unless you sell the property or refinance. SBA cash-out refinancing allows you to access a portion of that equity without giving up ownership, effectively turning a passive asset into an active source of capital.

One of the key principles of successful cash-out refinancing is that the capital you extract should be used productively. Borrowing against your equity increases your debt, so it must be justified by the returns generated from the use of that capital. For example, if you use the funds to expand your business, purchase revenue-generating equipment, or improve your property to increase rental income, the additional income can offset the cost of the loan and create net positive cash flow. On the other hand, using the funds for non-productive purposes can weaken your financial position.

SBA programs, particularly the SBA 7(a), provide flexibility when it comes to cash-out refinancing. In many cases, borrowers can access equity for a variety of business purposes, including working capital, expansion, and debt consolidation. However, there are guidelines and limitations that must be followed. The refinancing must demonstrate a clear benefit to the borrower, and the use of funds must align with SBA requirements. Understanding these guidelines is essential to structuring a successful transaction. Loan-to-value ratio is one of the most important factors in determining how much equity you can access. SBA loans typically allow for high leverage, but there are limits to ensure that the loan remains secure. For example, if your property is valued at $2,000,000 and your current loan balance is $1,000,000, you may be able to refinance up to a certain percentage of the property's value, such as 80% or 90%, depending on the program and your qualifications. This means you could potentially access several hundred thousand dollars in equity while still maintaining a reasonable level of leverage.

Another critical consideration is the impact of cash-out refinancing on your monthly payments. While accessing equity provides immediate capital, it also increases your loan balance, which can affect your monthly obligation. However, this increase can often be offset by extending the loan term or securing a lower interest rate. The goal is to structure the loan in a way that maintains or improves your cash flow while still providing access to the capital you need.

Risk management plays a central role in cash-out refinancing. Taking on additional debt always involves some level of risk, so it is important to evaluate your ability to repay the loan under different scenarios. This includes considering potential changes in revenue, market conditions, and interest rates. By conducting a thorough analysis and building a margin of safety into your projections, you can reduce the likelihood of financial strain.

Another powerful use of cash-out refinancing is property improvement. Investing in renovations or upgrades can increase the value of your property and generate higher income. For example, upgrading a commercial space can attract higher-paying tenants or allow you to increase rents. This not only improves your cash flow but also enhances the long-term value of your asset. In this way, cash-out refinancing can create a cycle of growth, where borrowed capital leads to increased value and income.

Cash-out refinancing can also be used to acquire additional properties or expand your portfolio. By leveraging the equity in one property, you can create opportunities to invest in new assets without needing to save large amounts of cash. This strategy allows you to scale your investments more quickly and take advantage of market opportunities. However, it requires careful planning to ensure that each investment contributes positively to your overall financial position.

Timing is another important factor. Property values, interest rates, and business performance all influence the effectiveness of cash-out refinancing. Refinancing when property values are high and interest rates are favorable can maximize the amount of equity you can access while minimizing the cost of borrowing. Monitoring these factors and acting at the right time can significantly enhance the benefits of the transaction.

It is also important to consider the long-term implications of cash-out refinancing. While the immediate benefits can be substantial, the increased loan balance means that you will pay more interest over time. This makes it essential to evaluate the overall return on investment. If the capital you extract generates returns that exceed the additional interest cost, the refinancing can be highly advantageous. If not, it may not be the best strategy.

Finally, cash-out refinancing should be viewed as part of a broader financial strategy. It is not just about accessing capital—it is about using that capital to achieve specific goals. Whether those goals involve expanding your business, improving your property, or increasing your income, every decision should be aligned with your long-term vision. By approaching cash-out refinancing with a strategic mindset, you can turn your equity into a powerful engine for growth.

By the end of this chapter, you should have a clear understanding of how to evaluate and implement cash-out refinancing strategies. You will know how to assess your equity, structure your loan, and deploy your capital effectively. With the right approach, cash-out refinancing can become one of the most valuable tools in your financial toolkit.

Real-Life Math Example: Using Cash-Out Refinancing to Scale a Business

Consider a business owner named Daniel who owns a commercial office building valued at $3,000,000. His current loan balance is $1,500,000 at an interest rate of 7.5%, with 18 years remaining. His monthly payment is approximately $13,900. Over the years, the property has appreciated significantly, and Daniel has built substantial equity.

Daniel decides to explore SBA cash-out refinancing to fund the expansion of his consulting business. Based on SBA guidelines and his financial profile, he is approved for a new loan at 80% loan-to-value. This allows him to refinance up to $2,400,000. After paying off his existing $1,500,000 loan, he is able to access $900,000 in cash-out proceeds.

The new loan is structured as an SBA 7(a) loan with an interest rate of 6.75% and a 25-year term. His new monthly payment is approximately $16,600. This represents an increase of $2,700 compared to his previous payment of $13,900. However, the key to evaluating this transaction lies in how Daniel uses the $900,000.

Daniel invests $500,000 into expanding his business operations, including hiring additional staff, upgrading technology, and increasing marketing efforts. This investment increases his monthly revenue by $25,000. He allocates another $200,000 to renovate the office building, allowing him to increase rental income by $6,000 per month. The remaining $200,000 is used as working capital to support the growth of his business.

Now let's analyze the financial impact. Daniel's total increase in monthly income is $31,000 ($25,000 from business expansion and $6,000 from increased rental income). His monthly loan payment increases by $2,700, resulting in a net monthly gain of $28,300. This dramatically improves his cash flow and provides a strong return on the capital he accessed.

Over time, the additional income generated from his investments far exceeds the cost of the additional debt. Even though his total loan payments over 25 years will be higher due to the increased loan amount and extended term, the net benefit to his business and financial position is substantial.

Additionally, Daniel's property value increases due to the renovations, further enhancing his equity position. His business growth also strengthens his financial profile, making it easier to qualify for future financing. This creates a compounding effect, where one strategic refinancing leads to multiple opportunities for growth. This example illustrates the true power of cash-out refinancing when used strategically. By leveraging his equity and investing the capital into high-return opportunities, Daniel transforms his financial position and accelerates his business growth. The key takeaway is that cash-out refinancing is not just about accessing money—it is about using that money to create value that exceeds the cost of borrowing.

Chapter 6

Reducing Risk and Stabilizing Your Business with SBA Refinancing

One of the most overlooked advantages of SBA commercial mortgage refinancing is its ability to reduce risk and bring long-term stability to a business. While many business owners focus on lowering payments or accessing capital, the deeper value of refinancing lies in creating predictability, protecting against market volatility, and strengthening the financial foundation of the business. In uncertain economic environments, businesses that prioritize stability often outperform those that operate with high levels of financial risk. In this chapter, you will learn how SBA refinancing can be used as a powerful risk management tool, how to identify hidden risks in your current debt structure, and how to design a loan strategy that protects your business over time.

Risk in commercial financing often comes from uncertainty. This uncertainty can take many forms, including variable interest rates, short-term loan maturities, high monthly payments, and complex debt structures. Each of these factors can create pressure on your cash flow and limit your ability to plan for the future. SBA refinancing addresses these issues by offering longer loan terms, more predictable payment structures, and the opportunity to consolidate multiple debts into a single, manageable obligation. By reducing uncertainty, you create a more stable environment in which your business can operate and grow.

One of the most significant sources of risk in commercial loans is variable interest rates. Many conventional commercial loans are tied to market benchmarks that fluctuate over time. While rates may be low initially, they can increase significantly, leading to higher monthly payments and unexpected financial strain. SBA refinancing, particularly through the SBA 504 program, allows borrowers to secure fixed-rate financing for extended periods. This stability eliminates the uncertainty associated with rate fluctuations and provides a consistent payment structure that can be relied upon for years to come.

Another major risk factor is loan maturity and balloon payments. Many commercial loans are structured with relatively short terms, such as five or ten years, with a large balloon payment due at the end of the term. This creates refinancing risk, as the borrower must secure new financing or pay off the remaining balance when the loan matures. If market conditions are unfavorable or the borrower's financial situation has changed, this can become a significant challenge. SBA loans, with their fully amortizing structures and long terms, eliminate the need for balloon payments, reducing the risk of future refinancing under uncertain conditions.

Cash flow volatility is another area where SBA refinancing can provide stability. High monthly debt payments can strain your business, particularly during periods of lower revenue. By extending the loan term and reducing monthly payments, SBA refinancing can create a buffer that allows your business to absorb fluctuations in income. This improved cash flow stability can be critical during economic downturns or periods of transition, providing the flexibility needed to maintain operations and continue growing.

Debt complexity is another hidden source of risk. Many businesses operate with multiple loans, each with different terms, interest rates, and payment schedules. This complexity can make financial management more difficult and increase the likelihood of errors or missed payments. SBA refinancing allows you to consolidate these obligations into a single loan, simplifying your financial structure and reducing administrative burden. A simpler debt structure is easier to manage, easier to monitor, and less prone to complications.

Leverage risk is also an important consideration. While leverage can be a powerful tool for growth, excessive debt can increase vulnerability, particularly if revenue declines or expenses increase. SBA refinancing provides an opportunity to restructure your leverage in a way that aligns with your cash flow capacity. By balancing loan-to-value ratios with income generation, you can maintain an appropriate level of leverage while reducing the risk of financial strain.

Another key concept is building a margin of safety. This involves structuring your loan in a way that allows your business to withstand unexpected challenges. For example, if your new loan reduces your monthly payments significantly, the difference can serve as a financial cushion. This cushion can be used to cover unexpected expenses, invest in opportunities, or simply provide peace of mind. A strong margin of safety is one of the most effective ways to reduce risk and ensure long-term sustainability.

Interest rate forecasting and economic awareness also play a role in risk management. While it is impossible to predict future market conditions with certainty, understanding trends and potential scenarios can help you make more informed decisions. For example, locking in a fixed rate during a period of rising interest rates can protect your business from future increases. Conversely, choosing a variable rate during a stable or declining rate environment may provide cost savings. The key is to align your strategy with your expectations and risk tolerance. Another important aspect of risk reduction is aligning your debt with your business lifecycle. Different stages of a business require different financial strategies. Early-stage businesses may prioritize flexibility and access to capital, while more established businesses may focus on stability and predictability. SBA refinancing allows you to adjust your debt structure as your business evolves, ensuring that your financing remains aligned with your needs.

Contingency planning is also essential. Even with a well-structured loan, unexpected events can occur. Having a plan in place for how you will respond to changes in revenue, expenses, or market conditions can help you navigate challenges more effectively. SBA refinancing can support this planning by providing a stable financial foundation, making it easier to anticipate and manage potential risks.

Finally, it is important to recognize that reducing risk is not about eliminating opportunity. In fact, a stable financial foundation often creates more opportunities by allowing you to take calculated risks with confidence. When your debt is structured effectively, your cash flow is predictable, and your financial position is strong, you are better equipped to pursue growth and expansion.

By the end of this chapter, you should have a clear understanding of how SBA refinancing can be used to reduce risk and stabilize your business. You will be able to identify potential risks in your current debt structure, evaluate your options, and design a refinancing strategy that enhances both stability and opportunity. With the right approach, SBA refinancing can become a cornerstone of your long-term financial strategy.

Real-Life Math Example: Using SBA Refinancing to Reduce Risk and Stabilize Cash Flow

Consider a business owner named Olivia who owns a retail distribution company and a commercial property valued at $2,200,000. She currently has a commercial loan balance of $1,300,000 with a variable interest rate of 7% that adjusts annually. Her loan has a remaining term of 10 years with a balloon payment at the end. Her current monthly payment is approximately $15,100, but she knows that this payment could increase if interest rates rise.

In addition to her mortgage, Olivia has $200,000 in short-term business debt with an average interest rate of 11%, resulting in monthly payments of $5,200. Her total monthly debt obligation is $20,300. Her business generates an average monthly income of $26,000, giving her a DSCR of approximately 1.28. While this meets minimum requirements, it leaves little room for unexpected changes. Olivia decides to refinance using an SBA 504 loan for the real estate and an SBA 7(a) loan to consolidate her short-term debt. For simplicity, let's focus on a combined restructuring approach equivalent to a single SBA solution. She refinances her total debt of $1,500,000 into a new loan with a blended interest rate of 6.25% and a 25-year term. Her new monthly payment is approximately $9,900.

This reduces her monthly debt obligation by $10,400 compared to her previous $20,300. Her new DSCR improves significantly. With her income remaining at $26,000 and her new debt payment at $9,900, her DSCR increases to approximately 2.63. This represents a substantial improvement in her financial stability.

Now let's consider the risk reduction. Previously, Olivia faced the possibility of rising interest rates increasing her payments, as well as the need to refinance or pay off a large balloon payment in 10 years. With the new SBA loan, her interest rate is fixed or stabilized, and her loan is fully amortizing over 25 years. This eliminates both the interest rate risk and the balloon payment risk.

Additionally, the $10,400 in monthly savings provides a significant financial cushion. Even if her business income were to decline by $8,000 per month, she would still be able to cover her loan payments comfortably. This margin of safety allows her to operate with greater confidence and reduces the likelihood of financial stress during challenging periods. Over time, Olivia uses a portion of her monthly savings to build a reserve fund. Within two years, she accumulates over $200,000 in reserves, further strengthening her financial position. This reserve can be used to manage unexpected expenses, invest in opportunities, or provide additional security.

This example demonstrates how SBA refinancing can transform a high-risk financial structure into a stable and predictable one. By reducing her monthly payments, eliminating variable rate exposure, and removing the balloon payment risk, Olivia significantly improves her financial security. The result is not just better cash flow, but a stronger, more resilient business capable of navigating uncertainty and pursuing growth with confidence.

Chapter 7

Timing the Market – When to Refinance for Maximum Advantage

Timing is one of the most critical yet overlooked elements of SBA commercial mortgage loan refinancing. While structure, qualification, and strategy all matter, the timing of your refinance can significantly influence the outcome. Refinancing at the right moment can maximize savings, increase access to equity, and strengthen your overall financial position. Refinancing at the wrong time, however, can limit benefits, increase costs, or reduce flexibility. In this chapter, you will learn how to identify the optimal time to refinance, how to evaluate market conditions, and how to align timing with your business goals to achieve maximum advantage.

One of the most important factors in timing a refinance is interest rates. Interest rates are constantly fluctuating based on economic conditions, inflation, and monetary policy. When rates are lower than the rate on your existing loan, refinancing can provide immediate savings through reduced interest costs and lower monthly payments. However, timing is not just about chasing the lowest possible rate–it is about understanding trends and acting strategically. Waiting too long in hopes of slightly lower rates can result in missed opportunities if rates begin to rise.

Economic cycles play a major role in interest rate movements. During periods of economic expansion, rates may increase as demand for capital grows and inflation pressures build. During economic slowdowns, rates may decrease as policymakers attempt to stimulate growth. Understanding where you are in the economic cycle can help you anticipate rate movements and make more informed decisions. While it is impossible to predict the future with certainty, being aware of these patterns allows you to act proactively rather than reactively.

Another critical timing factor is property value. The value of your commercial property directly impacts your loan-to-value ratio and the amount of equity you can access. When property values are high, you may be able to refinance at a higher valuation, allowing you to extract more equity or secure better terms. Conversely, if property values decline, your refinancing options may become more limited. Monitoring market trends and obtaining updated valuations can help you determine whether it is the right time to refinance.

Business performance is equally important. Lenders evaluate your financials at the time of application, so refinancing during a period of strong revenue and profitability can improve your chances of approval and help you secure better terms. If your business has recently experienced growth, increased cash flow, or improved financial metrics, this may be an ideal time to refinance. On the other hand, if your business is experiencing temporary challenges, it may be beneficial to wait until your financials stabilize.

Debt maturity is another key consideration. Many commercial loans have fixed terms with balloon payments due at the end. Waiting until the last minute to refinance can create unnecessary pressure and limit your options. Ideally, you should begin evaluating refinancing opportunities well before your loan matures, allowing you to take advantage of favorable conditions and avoid being forced into a decision under time constraints.

Prepayment penalties also influence timing decisions. Some loans include penalties for early repayment, particularly within the first few years. Understanding the structure of these penalties is essential when determining whether refinancing makes financial sense. In some cases, the savings from refinancing may outweigh the cost of the penalty. In other cases, it may be more advantageous to wait until the penalty period expires.

Another important concept is opportunity cost. Every financial decision involves trade-offs, and refinancing is no exception.

Delaying a refinance may allow you to secure a slightly better rate, but it also means continuing to operate under your current loan terms, which may be less favorable. Evaluating the opportunity cost of waiting versus acting now can help you make a more informed decision.

Market competition among lenders can also impact timing. During certain periods, lenders may be more aggressive in offering competitive terms to attract borrowers. This can create opportunities to secure better rates, lower fees, or more flexible terms. Staying informed about market conditions and maintaining relationships with lenders can help you identify these opportunities.

Another strategic consideration is aligning refinancing with your business goals. For example, if you are planning to expand your business, acquire new assets, or invest in growth opportunities, refinancing can provide the capital needed to execute those plans. Timing your refinance to coincide with these initiatives can enhance their effectiveness and maximize their impact.

Interest rate spreads and loan structures also play a role in timing. SBA loans are often tied to benchmark rates, such as the prime rate, plus a spread determined by the lender. Understanding how these components interact can help you evaluate whether current rates are favorable relative to historical trends. This knowledge allows you to make more strategic decisions about when to lock in a rate.

Another key factor is inflation. Inflation affects both interest rates and property values, influencing the overall economics of refinancing. During periods of higher inflation, borrowing at a fixed rate can be advantageous, as the real cost of debt decreases over time. Conversely, during periods of low inflation, the benefits of refinancing may be less pronounced. Understanding the relationship between inflation and financing can provide additional insight into timing decisions.

Stress-testing your refinancing scenario is another valuable tool. By modeling different outcomes based on changes in interest rates, income, and expenses, you can evaluate how your refinancing decision will perform under various conditions. This helps you identify potential risks and ensure that your decision remains sound even if circumstances change.

Finally, it is important to recognize that perfect timing is rarely achievable. The goal is not to predict the exact bottom of interest rates or the peak of property values, but to make a well-informed decision based on the information available. Taking a proactive approach and acting when conditions are favorable can often yield better results than waiting indefinitely for the "perfect" moment.

By the end of this chapter, you will have a clear understanding of how to evaluate timing in the context of SBA refinancing. You will be able to analyze interest rates, market conditions, business performance, and other key factors to determine when to act. With this knowledge, you can make strategic decisions that maximize the benefits of refinancing and support your long-term goals.

Real-Life Math Example: Timing an SBA Refinance for Maximum Financial Advantage

Consider a business owner named Victor who owns a commercial property valued at $2,400,000. He currently has a loan balance of $1,400,000 at an interest rate of 8%, with 12 years remaining. His monthly payment is approximately $15,400. Over the past year, interest rates have declined, and Victor is considering refinancing into an SBA loan.

At the time Victor begins evaluating his options, SBA loan rates are approximately 6.5%. If he refinances immediately into a 25-year SBA loan at 6.5%, his new monthly payment would be approximately $9,500. This represents a monthly savings of $5,900 compared to his current payment.

However, Victor considers waiting, hoping that rates will decline further to 6%. If rates drop to 6%, his monthly payment would be approximately $9,000, saving an additional $500 per month compared to refinancing at 6.5%. While this may seem beneficial, waiting introduces risk.

Let's analyze the opportunity cost. If Victor refinances now, he begins saving $5,900 per month immediately. Over the next 12 months, this results in total savings of $70,800. If he waits one year for rates to potentially drop to 6%, he forgoes these savings. Even if he achieves the lower rate, the additional $500 per month savings would take over 11 years to recover the $70,800 lost during the waiting period.

Additionally, there is no guarantee that rates will decrease. If rates increase instead, Victor could miss the opportunity to refinance at a favorable rate altogether. For example, if rates rise to 7%, his new monthly payment would be approximately $10,700, reducing his potential savings.

Now consider property value. During this period, Victor's property appreciates from $2,400,000 to $2,600,000. If he refinances after this increase, he may be able to access additional equity. At 80% loan-to-value, he could refinance up to $2,080,000, compared to $1,920,000 previously. This provides an additional $160,000 in potential cash-out.

However, this benefit must be weighed against the opportunity cost of delaying the refinance. If Victor uses the additional equity to invest in his business and generate returns, the delay may be justified. If not, the lost savings from waiting may outweigh the benefits.

Ultimately, Victor decides to refinance immediately, locking in a 6.5% rate and securing monthly savings of $5,900. He also gains stability with a long-term loan structure and uses a portion of his savings to invest in his business, generating additional income.

This example demonstrates the importance of timing in refinancing decisions. By evaluating interest rates, opportunity cost, and market conditions, Victor is able to make a strategic decision that maximizes his financial advantage. The key takeaway is that timing is not about perfection—it is about making informed decisions that align with your goals and the opportunities available in the moment.

Chapter 8

Using SBA Refinancing to Scale – Building a Portfolio and Expanding Your Business

One of the most powerful outcomes of SBA commercial mortgage refinancing is its ability to serve as a launchpad for growth. While many business owners initially pursue refinancing to reduce payments or stabilize their financial position, the true long-term value often lies in how refinancing can be leveraged to scale operations, acquire additional properties, and build a portfolio of income-producing assets. In this chapter, you will learn how to transition from using SBA refinancing as a defensive strategy to using it as an offensive growth tool, allowing you to expand your business, multiply your assets, and accelerate your path to financial independence.

At its core, scaling through SBA refinancing is about creating a repeatable system. The process begins with improving your existing financial position—reducing monthly payments, increasing cash flow, and strengthening your balance sheet. Once this foundation is in place, you can begin to leverage that improved position to pursue new opportunities. This might include acquiring additional commercial properties, expanding your current business operations, or investing in new ventures. Each successful refinancing strengthens your ability to take the next step, creating a compounding effect over time.

The first principle of scaling is cash flow optimization. Cash flow is what fuels growth, and SBA refinancing can significantly enhance it by lowering your monthly debt obligations. The difference between your old and new payments becomes available capital that can be reinvested into your business. This reinvestment is what drives expansion, allowing you to generate additional income that further strengthens your financial position. The key is to treat your savings not as extra spending money, but as growth capital that can be deployed strategically.

Another important concept is equity recycling. As your properties appreciate in value and your loan balances decrease, you build equity. Through refinancing, you can access a portion of that equity and use it to fund new investments. This allows you to grow your portfolio without relying solely on savings or external capital. By continuously reinvesting your equity into new opportunities, you create a cycle of growth that can significantly accelerate your progress.

Portfolio building requires a disciplined approach. Each acquisition or expansion should be evaluated based on its ability to generate positive cash flow and contribute to your overall strategy. SBA refinancing provides the capital and flexibility needed to pursue these opportunities, but it is up to you to ensure that each decision aligns with your long-term goals. This means analyzing potential investments carefully, understanding the risks involved, and ensuring that each move strengthens your financial position.

Leverage plays a central role in scaling. By using borrowed capital to acquire or improve assets, you can achieve growth that would be difficult or impossible with cash alone. SBA programs allow for relatively high leverage, making it possible to control valuable assets with a smaller initial investment. However, leverage must be used responsibly. The goal is to create a balance where your assets generate enough income to cover your debt obligations while still producing positive cash flow.

Another key factor is diversification. As you build your portfolio, it is important to spread your investments across different types of assets or income streams. This reduces risk and creates multiple sources of revenue. SBA refinancing can support diversification by providing the capital needed to explore new opportunities, whether that involves different types of properties, new business ventures, or complementary investments. Scaling also requires a strong understanding of timing and market conditions. Identifying opportunities when they are undervalued or when financing conditions are favorable can significantly enhance your returns. SBA refinancing provides the flexibility to act when these opportunities arise, allowing you to move quickly and capitalize on favorable conditions.

Operational efficiency is another important component of scaling. As your business grows, managing multiple properties or operations can become more complex. Streamlining your processes, implementing systems, and maintaining strong financial controls are essential to sustaining growth. SBA refinancing can support these efforts by providing the capital needed to invest in technology, personnel, and infrastructure.

Risk management remains critical as you scale. While growth creates opportunities, it also introduces new challenges. Ensuring that your debt levels remain manageable, maintaining adequate reserves, and continuously monitoring your financial performance are all essential to long-term success. SBA refinancing can help mitigate risk by providing stable, predictable financing, but it must be combined with disciplined management.

Another powerful aspect of scaling is compounding. Each successful investment generates additional income, which can be reinvested into further opportunities. Over time, this creates exponential growth. SBA refinancing acts as a catalyst for this process by unlocking capital and improving cash flow, allowing you to accelerate your progress.

It is also important to align your scaling strategy with your personal and professional goals. Whether you aim to build a large real estate portfolio, expand your business operations, or create passive income streams, your refinancing strategy should support those objectives. This alignment ensures that your growth is intentional and sustainable.

Finally, scaling through SBA refinancing requires a long-term perspective. While the immediate benefits of refinancing are important, the true value lies in how those benefits are used over time. By consistently reinvesting your savings and equity into productive opportunities, you can build a portfolio that generates increasing levels of income and value.

By the end of this chapter, you will understand how to use SBA refinancing as a tool for scaling your business and building a portfolio of assets. You will be equipped with the strategies needed to optimize cash flow, recycle equity, and create a system for continuous growth. With the right approach, SBA refinancing can become the foundation of a powerful and sustainable growth strategy.

Real-Life Math Example: Scaling a Business and Portfolio Using SBA Refinancing

Consider a business owner named Javier who owns a commercial property valued at $2,000,000 with a current loan balance of $1,200,000 at an interest rate of 7.5%. His monthly payment is approximately $12,000. Javier refinances using an SBA 7(a) loan at 6.5% over 25 years, resulting in a new monthly payment of approximately $8,100. This reduces his monthly payment by $3,900.

Javier decides to use this $3,900 in monthly savings as growth capital. Over the course of one year, he accumulates $46,800. In addition, his property appreciates to $2,200,000, increasing his available equity. He performs a cash-out refinance and accesses $200,000, which he combines with his savings to invest in a second property.

The second property costs $600,000 and generates $6,000 in monthly rental income. Javier finances 80% of the purchase price, resulting in a loan of $480,000 with a monthly payment of approximately $3,200. After accounting for expenses and debt service, the property generates a net cash flow of $2,800 per month.

Now Javier's total monthly improvement includes his original savings of $3,900 plus the $2,800 from the new property, resulting in $6,700 in additional monthly cash flow. Over the next two years, he continues this strategy, using his increased income to acquire a third property.

The third property costs $800,000 and generates $8,000 in monthly rental income. With similar financing, his net cash flow from this property is $3,500 per month. At this point, Javier's total additional monthly cash flow is $10,200.

Over time, this compounding effect continues. Each new property generates income that can be reinvested into further opportunities. After five years, Javier owns multiple properties generating over $20,000 in additional monthly cash flow. His original refinancing decision has evolved into a scalable system that drives continuous growth.

This example demonstrates how SBA refinancing can be used as a foundation for scaling. By optimizing cash flow, accessing equity, and reinvesting strategically, Javier transforms his financial position and builds a portfolio of income-producing assets. The key takeaway is that refinancing is not just about improving your current situation—it is about creating opportunities for future growth and leveraging them effectively.

Chapter 9

Avoiding Common Mistakes in SBA Refinancing — Protecting Your Deal and Your Future

SBA commercial mortgage refinancing can be one of the most powerful financial strategies available to business owners, but like any powerful tool, it must be used correctly. Many borrowers focus on the benefits—lower payments, improved cash flow, access to capital—but overlook the potential pitfalls that can reduce or even eliminate those advantages. The difference between a successful refinancing and a costly mistake often lies in the details: how the deal is structured, how the funds are used, and how the borrower plans for the future. In this chapter, you will learn how to identify and avoid the most common mistakes in SBA refinancing, ensuring that your transaction strengthens your financial position rather than weakening it.

One of the most common mistakes is focusing solely on the monthly payment while ignoring the total cost of the loan. Lower monthly payments are attractive and often necessary for improving cash flow, but they are usually achieved by extending the loan term. This can result in significantly higher total interest paid over time. While this trade-off can be justified if the improved cash flow is used productively, it becomes a problem when borrowers fail to evaluate the long-term cost. The key is to balance short-term relief with long-term efficiency, ensuring that the benefits outweigh the additional expense.

Another frequent mistake is overleveraging. SBA loans allow for relatively high loan-to-value ratios, which can make it tempting to borrow as much as possible. While accessing equity can be beneficial, taking on too much debt can increase financial risk and reduce flexibility. If your business experiences a downturn or unexpected expenses arise, high debt levels can create significant pressure. A disciplined approach to leverage ensures that your debt remains manageable and aligned with your cash flow capacity.

Misusing cash-out funds is another critical error. Cash-out refinancing provides access to capital, but how that capital is used determines whether the transaction is successful. Using the funds for non-productive purposes—such as covering ongoing losses or personal expenses—can weaken your financial position. In contrast, investing the funds into revenue-generating activities, such as expansion, equipment, or property improvements, can create returns that exceed the cost of borrowing. Every dollar extracted through refinancing should have a clear purpose and a measurable impact.

Failing to understand loan terms is another common issue. SBA loans come with specific structures, including interest rate types, amortization schedules, and potential prepayment penalties. Borrowers who do not fully understand these terms may find themselves facing unexpected costs or limitations. For example, prepayment penalties can impact your ability to refinance again or pay off the loan early. Taking the time to understand the details of your loan ensures that there are no surprises down the road.

Another mistake is poor timing. Refinancing at the wrong time—such as during a period of declining business performance or unfavorable market conditions—can limit your options and reduce the benefits of the transaction. While it is impossible to perfectly time the market, being aware of key factors such as interest rates, property values, and business performance can help you make more informed decisions. Acting proactively rather than reactively often leads to better outcomes.

Inadequate preparation is another factor that can derail a refinancing. SBA loans require detailed documentation and thorough underwriting. Borrowers who are unprepared may face delays, additional scrutiny, or even denial. Ensuring that your financials are accurate, your documentation is complete, and your business narrative is clear can significantly improve your chances of approval and streamline the process.

Another overlooked mistake is failing to align refinancing with long-term goals. Refinancing should not be viewed as a standalone transaction—it should be part of a broader financial strategy. Whether your goal is to expand your business, build a portfolio, or improve stability, your refinancing structure should support those objectives. Without this alignment, you may find that your loan terms do not fully support your plans.

Ignoring risk is another critical issue. While SBA refinancing can reduce many types of risk, it does not eliminate risk entirely. Borrowers must still consider factors such as changes in revenue, economic conditions, and interest rates. Building a margin of safety into your financial planning—such as maintaining reserves or structuring conservative payments—can help mitigate these risks and ensure long-term sustainability.

Another mistake is neglecting to monitor performance after refinancing. The work does not end once the loan is closed. Tracking your financial performance, evaluating the impact of your refinancing, and making adjustments as needed are essential to maximizing the benefits. This ongoing management ensures that your refinancing continues to support your goals over time. Working with the wrong team can also lead to suboptimal outcomes. SBA refinancing involves multiple parties, including lenders, brokers, and advisors. Choosing experienced professionals who understand the nuances of SBA programs can make a significant difference in the quality of your deal. A knowledgeable team can help you structure your loan effectively, avoid common pitfalls, and navigate the process with confidence.

Another important consideration is understanding opportunity cost. Every financial decision involves trade-offs, and refinancing is no exception. Choosing one structure or strategy may limit your ability to pursue other opportunities. Evaluating these trade-offs ensures that you are making decisions that align with your priorities and maximize your overall benefit.

Finally, it is important to maintain discipline and perspective. Refinancing is a powerful tool, but it is not a shortcut to success. It requires careful planning, thoughtful execution, and ongoing management. By avoiding the common mistakes outlined in this chapter, you can ensure that your refinancing strengthens your financial position and supports your long-term goals.

By the end of this chapter, you will have a clear understanding of the potential pitfalls in SBA refinancing and how to avoid them. You will be equipped with the knowledge and strategies needed to protect your deal, optimize your results, and build a strong foundation for future growth.

Real-Life Math Example: Avoiding Costly Mistakes in SBA Refinancing

Consider a business owner named Anthony who owns a commercial property valued at $2,800,000. His current loan balance is $1,600,000 at an interest rate of 8%, with 15 years remaining. His monthly payment is approximately $15,300. Anthony decides to refinance using an SBA 7(a) loan to reduce his payments and access equity.

He is approved for a new loan of $2,200,000 at an interest rate of 6.75% over 25 years. This includes paying off his existing loan and providing $600,000 in cash-out. His new monthly payment is approximately $15,200, which is slightly lower than his previous payment despite the higher loan amount.

At first glance, this seems like a successful refinance. However, let's examine how Anthony uses the $600,000. Instead of investing it into his business or income-generating assets, he uses $400,000 for personal expenses and $200,000 to cover operating losses. As a result, he does not generate any additional income from the cash-out funds.

Now let's analyze the long-term impact. Under his original loan, Anthony would have paid approximately $2,754,000 over the remaining term. With the new loan, his total payments over 25 years will be approximately $4,560,000. This represents a significant increase in total cost due to the larger loan amount and extended term.

Since Anthony did not use the cash-out funds productively, he does not generate additional income to offset this cost. His monthly cash flow remains largely unchanged, but his long-term financial obligation has increased significantly. This illustrates the risk of misusing cash-out funds.

Now consider an alternative scenario. If Anthony had invested the $600,000 into his business and generated an additional $12,000 per month in revenue, his financial position would look very different. With his new loan payment of $15,200 and additional income of $12,000, his net cash flow would improve significantly.

Over time, the additional income would offset the increased cost of the loan, making the refinancing a strategic success.

This comparison highlights the importance of how cash-out funds are used.

Another mistake Anthony could have avoided is overleveraging. By borrowing $2,200,000 on a $2,800,000 property, his loan-to-value ratio is approximately 79%. While this is within acceptable limits, it leaves less room for error if property values decline. A more conservative approach—such as borrowing less and maintaining a lower loan-to-value ratio—could provide greater stability.

Additionally, Anthony did not fully consider the long-term cost of his loan. While his monthly payment remained similar, the extended term resulted in significantly higher total interest. Evaluating both short-term and long-term impacts could have helped him make a more informed decision.

This example demonstrates how common mistakes in SBA refinancing can impact your financial outcome. By focusing on both immediate benefits and long-term consequences, using funds productively, and maintaining a disciplined approach, you can avoid these pitfalls and maximize the value of your refinancing.

Chapter 10

Building a Long-Term Exit Strategy with SBA Refinancing

Refinancing is not just about improving your present—it is about shaping your future. The most successful business owners and investors understand that every financial decision should align with a long-term exit strategy. Whether your goal is to sell your business, transition into passive income, pass assets to your family, or simply achieve financial independence, SBA commercial mortgage refinancing can play a critical role in helping you get there. In this chapter, you will learn how to use refinancing as a strategic tool to design and execute a long-term exit plan that maximizes value, minimizes risk, and creates lasting wealth.

The concept of an exit strategy begins with clarity. You must define what "exit" means for you. For some, it means selling a business and realizing a lump sum of capital. For others, it means building a portfolio of income-producing assets that provide ongoing passive income. In some cases, it may involve transitioning ownership to family members or partners. Each of these outcomes requires a different financial approach, and your refinancing strategy should be tailored accordingly. One of the most important principles in building an exit strategy is cash flow stability. Buyers, investors, and successors all place a high value on predictable income. SBA refinancing can help you achieve this by converting short-term or variable-rate debt into long-term, stable financing. This predictability enhances the attractiveness of your business or property, making it easier to sell or transfer at a higher valuation.

Valuation is another key component of your exit strategy. The value of a business or property is often tied to its income and financial structure. Lower debt payments and improved cash flow can increase net income, which in turn can increase valuation. By refinancing to reduce your monthly obligations, you can enhance your financial metrics and position your asset for a more favorable exit.

Debt structure also plays a significant role in exit planning. Complex or high-risk debt can deter potential buyers or complicate a transition. SBA refinancing allows you to simplify your financial structure, consolidate debt, and create a more attractive profile. A clean, well-structured balance sheet is easier to evaluate and more appealing to buyers.

Another important concept is equity positioning. As you refinance and pay down your loan over time, your equity increases. This equity represents your ownership stake and the value you can realize upon exit. Strategic refinancing can help you manage your equity in a way that aligns with your goals, whether that involves building maximum equity for a sale or leveraging equity to generate ongoing income.

Timing your exit is also critical. Just as timing matters in refinancing, it also matters in exiting. Market conditions, interest rates, and business performance all influence the value you can achieve. SBA refinancing can provide the stability needed to wait for the right moment, allowing you to exit when conditions are most favorable rather than being forced to act under pressure.

Another strategy is transitioning from active income to passive income. Many business owners reach a point where they want to reduce their involvement while maintaining their income. SBA refinancing can support this transition by improving cash flow and reducing financial stress, making it easier to step back from day-to-day operations. This can be particularly valuable for those looking to retire or focus on other ventures.

Portfolio exit strategies are also important for those who have scaled their investments. Instead of selling all assets at once, you may choose to exit gradually, selling properties or businesses over time. SBA refinancing can support this approach by stabilizing your financing and providing flexibility as you transition. Tax considerations are another critical aspect of exit planning. The way your assets are structured and financed can impact your tax liability upon sale or transfer. While specific tax strategies should be discussed with professionals, understanding the general implications can help you make more informed decisions. SBA refinancing can influence these outcomes by changing your debt structure and cash flow.

Succession planning is another area where refinancing can play a role. If you plan to pass your business or properties to family members or partners, having a stable and manageable debt structure can make the transition smoother. SBA refinancing can help create a financial environment that supports continuity and long-term success.

Another important factor is liquidity. An effective exit strategy often requires access to cash, whether for reinvestment, retirement, or other purposes. Cash-out refinancing can provide liquidity without requiring a sale, allowing you to access capital while maintaining ownership. This can be particularly useful as part of a phased exit strategy.

Risk reduction remains essential throughout the exit process. As you approach your exit, reducing exposure to market volatility and financial uncertainty becomes increasingly important. SBA refinancing can help achieve this by providing stable, long-term financing that minimizes risk.

Legacy building is another consideration. For many business owners, the goal is not just financial success but also creating something that lasts. Whether that involves building a portfolio, supporting family members, or contributing to the community, your refinancing strategy can support these objectives by providing the financial foundation needed to sustain your vision.

Finally, it is important to approach your exit strategy with flexibility. Circumstances can change, and your plans may evolve over time. SBA refinancing provides the adaptability needed to adjust your strategy as needed, ensuring that you remain aligned with your goals.

By the end of this chapter, you will have a comprehensive understanding of how SBA refinancing can support your long-term exit strategy. You will be able to align your financial decisions with your goals, optimize your assets for maximum value, and create a plan that ensures a successful transition.

Real-Life Math Example: Using SBA Refinancing to Build and Execute an Exit Strategy

Consider a business owner named Laura who owns a commercial property and business valued together at $3,500,000. She has an existing loan balance of $2,000,000 at an interest rate of 7.75%, with 15 years remaining. Her monthly payment is approximately $18,900. Her business generates net income of $30,000 per month.

Laura plans to exit her business within the next 10 years and wants to maximize its value while reducing her involvement over time. She decides to refinance using an SBA 504 loan, securing a fixed interest rate of 6.25% over 25 years. Her new monthly payment is approximately $13,200, reducing her payment by $5,700 per month.

This reduction in debt service increases her net income from $30,000 to $35,700 per month. Over time, this improved cash flow enhances the value of her business. If her business is valued at a multiple of 6 times annual net income, her valuation increases significantly.

Before refinancing, her annual net income was $360,000, resulting in a valuation of $2,160,000. After refinancing, her annual net income increases to $428,400, resulting in a valuation of approximately $2,570,400. This represents an increase of over $400,000 in value simply from improving her financial structure.

Over the next 10 years, Laura continues to pay down her loan while benefiting from stable payments and increased cash flow. Her loan balance decreases to approximately

$1,400,000, while her property value increases to $4,200,000. Her equity grows to $2,800,000.

When she decides to exit, Laura sells her business and property for $4,200,000. After paying off her remaining loan of $1,400,000, she realizes $2,800,000 in proceeds. Combined with the additional cash flow she generated over the years, her total financial benefit is substantial.

Additionally, the stability provided by her SBA loan made her business more attractive to buyers, allowing her to secure a higher valuation and a smoother transaction. Her ability to demonstrate consistent cash flow and a well-structured financial profile played a key role in achieving this outcome.

This example illustrates how SBA refinancing can be used as a strategic tool to build and execute a long-term exit plan. By improving cash flow, increasing valuation, and reducing risk, Laura is able to maximize the value of her business and achieve her financial goals.

Chapter 11

Advanced SBA Refinancing Strategies – Layering, Hybrid Structures, and Capital Stacking

As you progress beyond the fundamentals of SBA refinancing, the next level of mastery involves combining multiple strategies into sophisticated structures that maximize efficiency, flexibility, and long-term returns. This is where advanced SBA refinancing comes into play. Instead of viewing refinancing as a single transaction, experienced business owners and investors begin to treat it as part of a broader financial system—one that integrates multiple loan types, capital sources, and timing strategies to create optimized outcomes. In this chapter, you will learn how to use advanced techniques such as layering, hybrid structures, and capital stacking to elevate your refinancing strategy and unlock new levels of growth.

Layering is one of the most powerful concepts in advanced refinancing. It involves combining different types of financing to achieve a specific objective. For example, you might use an SBA 504 loan to secure long-term, fixed-rate financing for your real estate, while simultaneously using an SBA 7(a) loan to refinance business debt or access working capital. Each loan serves a distinct purpose, and together they create a more efficient overall structure. This approach allows you to take advantage of the strengths of each program while minimizing their limitations.

Hybrid structures take layering a step further by integrating SBA loans with other forms of financing, such as conventional loans, lines of credit, or private capital. For instance, you might refinance your primary property using an SBA 504 loan while maintaining a separate line of credit for short-term needs. This combination provides both stability and flexibility, allowing you to manage your long-term obligations while retaining access to liquid capital. Hybrid structures are particularly useful for businesses with diverse financial needs that cannot be fully addressed by a single loan.

Capital stacking is another advanced strategy that involves combining multiple sources of capital to fund a project or refinance. This might include SBA loans, investor contributions, seller financing, or even internal funds. By stacking different types of capital, you can structure deals that would not be possible with a single funding source. For example, you might use SBA refinancing to stabilize your existing debt while bringing in additional capital to fund expansion or acquisitions. This approach allows you to leverage multiple resources to achieve your objectives. One of the key benefits of advanced refinancing strategies is increased flexibility. By using multiple layers of financing, you can tailor your structure to meet your specific needs. This might involve adjusting repayment terms, balancing fixed and variable rates, or allocating capital to different areas of your business. Flexibility is especially important in dynamic environments where conditions can change quickly.

Another advantage is risk diversification. By spreading your financing across different sources and structures, you reduce your exposure to any single risk factor. For example, combining fixed-rate and variable-rate loans can balance stability and cost efficiency. Similarly, using multiple lenders or programs can reduce dependency on a single source of capital. This diversification enhances your ability to manage risk and adapt to changing conditions.

Advanced refinancing also enables more efficient use of capital. By strategically allocating funds across different components of your business, you can maximize returns and minimize costs. For example, using lower-cost SBA financing for long-term assets while reserving higher-cost, flexible capital for short-term needs can improve overall efficiency. This targeted approach ensures that each dollar is used in the most effective way possible. Timing becomes even more critical in advanced strategies. Coordinating multiple transactions, aligning different financing sources, and optimizing market conditions require careful planning. Executing these strategies effectively often involves staging your refinancing over time, rather than completing everything at once. This phased approach allows you to adapt to changing conditions and optimize each step of the process.

Another important concept is scalability. Advanced refinancing strategies are designed to support growth at scale. By creating systems that can be replicated and expanded, you can continue to build your portfolio and increase your income over time. This might involve repeating successful structures across multiple properties or using refinancing to fund ongoing expansion. Scalability is what transforms individual transactions into a long-term growth strategy.

Cash flow management remains central to advanced refinancing. Each layer of financing must be evaluated based on its impact on your overall cash flow. The goal is to create a structure where your income comfortably exceeds your obligations, even as you add complexity. This requires careful analysis and ongoing monitoring to ensure that your strategy remains sustainable.

Another key factor is coordination. Advanced refinancing often involves multiple parties, including lenders, investors, and advisors. Effective communication and coordination are essential to ensuring that all components of your strategy work together seamlessly. This may involve aligning timelines, negotiating terms, and managing relationships across different stakeholders.

Documentation and compliance also become more complex as you move into advanced strategies. Each layer of financing may have its own requirements, and ensuring that all conditions are met is critical to the success of your deal. Working with experienced professionals can help you navigate these complexities and avoid potential issues.

Strategic vision is what ties everything together. Advanced refinancing is not just about combining different tools—it is about using those tools to achieve a clear and defined objective. Whether your goal is to build a large portfolio, create multiple income streams, or prepare for a future exit, your strategy should be guided by that vision.

Finally, it is important to maintain discipline. While advanced strategies offer significant opportunities, they also require a higher level of expertise and attention to detail. Avoiding unnecessary complexity, staying focused on your goals, and continuously evaluating your performance are essential to long-term success. By the end of this chapter, you will have a deep understanding of how to use advanced SBA refinancing strategies to optimize your financial structure and support your growth. You will be able to combine different types of financing, manage complexity, and create a system that drives long-term success.

Real-Life Math Example: Using Layering and Capital Stacking to Expand a Portfolio

Consider a business owner named Rafael who owns a commercial property valued at $3,200,000 with an existing loan balance of $1,800,000 at 7.5%. His monthly payment is approximately $16,800. Rafael also has $300,000 in business debt with monthly payments of $6,500, bringing his total monthly obligation to $23,300.

Rafael decides to implement an advanced refinancing strategy using both SBA 504 and SBA 7(a) loans. He refinances his real estate using an SBA 504 loan at a blended rate of 6.25% over 25 years, resulting in a new monthly payment of approximately $11,800 on the real estate portion. He then uses an SBA 7(a) loan to refinance his $300,000 in business debt at 6.75% over 10 years, resulting in a monthly payment of approximately $3,400.

His new total monthly obligation becomes $15,200, compared to his previous $23,300. This results in monthly savings of $8,100. Rafael uses this improved cash flow as part of a capital stacking strategy.

Over the course of one year, he accumulates $97,200 in savings. He also performs a partial cash-out refinance, accessing $250,000 in equity. He combines these funds with a $150,000 investment from a partner, creating a total capital pool of $497,200.

Rafael uses this capital to acquire a new commercial property for $1,200,000. He finances 75% of the purchase with a loan of $900,000 at a monthly payment of approximately $6,500. The property generates $12,000 in monthly rental income, resulting in net cash flow of $5,500 after debt service and expenses.

Now let's evaluate the overall impact. Rafael's original monthly savings from refinancing is $8,100, and his new property generates $5,500 in additional cash flow. This results in a total monthly improvement of $13,600.

Over time, Rafael repeats this strategy, using his increased cash flow and equity to acquire additional properties. After three years, he owns multiple properties generating over $25,000 in monthly cash flow.

This example demonstrates how advanced SBA refinancing strategies can be used to layer financing, stack capital, and scale a portfolio. By combining different loan types, leveraging equity, and partnering with investors, Rafael creates a system that drives continuous growth and maximizes his financial potential.

Chapter 12

Creating a Repeatable SBA Refinancing System — From One Deal to a Financial Machine

The ultimate goal of mastering SBA commercial mortgage refinancing is not just to complete a single successful transaction—it is to build a repeatable system that can be applied over and over again to generate consistent growth, increasing cash flow, and long-term wealth. The most successful business owners and investors do not rely on one deal; they develop a process that turns refinancing into a predictable, scalable financial machine. In this chapter, you will learn how to design, implement, and refine a repeatable SBA refinancing system that allows you to continuously improve your financial position and expand your portfolio.

A repeatable system begins with a clear framework. This framework includes identifying opportunities, evaluating financial metrics, structuring the deal, executing the refinance, and reinvesting the benefits. Each step must be defined and optimized so that it can be replicated with consistency. The goal is to remove uncertainty and create a process that can be followed regardless of the specific details of each transaction.

The first step in building this system is opportunity identification. This involves continuously analyzing your existing assets and financial structure to identify areas where refinancing can provide a benefit. This might include high-interest debt, short-term loans, or properties with significant equity. By regularly reviewing your financial position, you can identify opportunities before they become urgent, allowing you to act strategically rather than reactively.

The second step is financial analysis. Once an opportunity is identified, you must evaluate the potential impact of refinancing. This includes analyzing your current loan terms, calculating potential savings, and assessing how the new structure will affect your cash flow, leverage, and overall financial position. Developing a consistent method for performing this analysis ensures that you can quickly and accurately evaluate each opportunity.

The third step is deal structuring. This is where you design the refinancing to achieve your objectives. This may involve choosing between SBA 7(a) and SBA 504 programs, determining the appropriate loan amount, and deciding whether to include cash-out. A well-structured deal aligns with your goals and maximizes the benefits of refinancing. By standardizing your approach to structuring, you can streamline this process and improve outcomes.

Execution is the next step. This involves working with lenders, gathering documentation, and navigating the approval process. Having a clear checklist and a defined workflow can make this process more efficient and reduce the likelihood of delays or complications. Over time, as you complete more transactions, your execution process becomes faster and more refined.

Reinvestment is what transforms refinancing into a growth engine. The savings and capital generated from refinancing should be deployed strategically to create additional value. This might involve investing in new properties, expanding your business, or improving existing assets. The key is to ensure that each reinvestment contributes to your overall strategy and generates returns that exceed the cost of borrowing.

Another important component of a repeatable system is tracking and measurement. By monitoring the performance of each refinancing transaction, you can identify what works and what does not. This includes tracking metrics such as cash flow improvement, return on investment, and changes in financial ratios. This data allows you to refine your process and make more informed decisions over time.

Standardization is also critical. While each deal may have unique elements, having standardized processes, templates, and criteria can significantly improve efficiency. This might include standardized financial models, documentation checklists, and evaluation criteria. Standardization reduces variability and allows you to scale your system more effectively.

Automation can further enhance your system. Using tools and technology to automate repetitive tasks, such as financial analysis or document management, can save time and reduce errors. While not all aspects of refinancing can be automated, identifying areas where automation can be applied can improve efficiency and scalability.

Another key element is building a strong network. Relationships with lenders, brokers, and advisors can provide access to opportunities, insights, and resources that enhance your system. A reliable network can also help you execute transactions more efficiently and navigate challenges more effectively.

Risk management remains essential within a repeatable system. Each transaction should be evaluated not only for its potential benefits but also for its risks. Maintaining conservative assumptions, building reserves, and ensuring that your debt levels remain manageable are all critical to sustaining your system over the long term.

Scalability is what differentiates a system from a one-time strategy. A scalable system allows you to increase the number and size of your transactions without significantly increasing complexity. This requires careful planning, efficient processes, and the ability to manage multiple deals simultaneously.

Another important concept is compounding. Each successful refinancing and reinvestment generates additional income and equity, which can be used to fund future transactions. Over time, this creates exponential growth. The power of compounding is what transforms a series of individual deals into a long-term wealth-building strategy.

Adaptability is also crucial. Market conditions, interest rates, and business environments change over time. A successful system must be flexible enough to adapt to these changes while maintaining its core principles. This may involve adjusting your criteria, exploring new opportunities, or modifying your approach as needed.

Finally, discipline and consistency are the foundation of any successful system. Building a repeatable SBA refinancing process requires commitment and attention to detail. By consistently applying your framework and continuously refining your approach, you can create a system that delivers reliable results over time.

By the end of this chapter, you will have a clear understanding of how to build and operate a repeatable SBA refinancing system. You will be equipped with the tools and strategies needed to identify opportunities, execute transactions, and reinvest the benefits in a way that drives continuous growth. With the right system in place, refinancing becomes more than a financial tool—it becomes a powerful engine for long-term success.

Real-Life Math Example: Building a Repeatable SBA Refinancing System

Consider a business owner named Isabella who owns a commercial property valued at $1,800,000 with an existing loan balance of $1,100,000 at 7.5%. Her monthly payment is approximately $10,800. She refinances using an SBA 7(a) loan at 6.5% over 25 years, reducing her monthly payment to $7,400. This creates a monthly savings of $3,400.

Isabella uses this $3,400 as the foundation of her system. Over one year, she accumulates $40,800 in savings. She combines this with a $100,000 cash-out refinance, giving her $140,800 to invest in a second property.

The second property costs $500,000 and generates $5,000 in monthly rental income. She finances 80% of the purchase, resulting in a loan of $400,000 with a monthly payment of approximately $2,700. After expenses, the property generates net cash flow of $2,300 per month. Now Isabella's total monthly improvement is $3,400 from her original refinance plus $2,300 from the new property, totaling $5,700. Over the next year, she saves $68,400, which she uses along with additional equity to acquire a third property.

The third property costs $700,000 and generates $7,000 in monthly rental income. With similar financing, it produces net cash flow of $3,000 per month. Isabella's total additional monthly cash flow now reaches $8,700.

She continues this process, refinancing when beneficial, reinvesting her savings and equity, and acquiring new properties. After five years, Isabella owns multiple properties generating over $18,000 in additional monthly cash flow.

This example demonstrates how a repeatable SBA refinancing system can transform a single transaction into a powerful growth engine. By consistently applying the same process—refinancing, saving, reinvesting, and scaling—Isabella builds a portfolio that generates increasing income and long-term wealth.

Chapter 13

Mastering Cash Flow Engineering – Turning SBA Refinancing into Predictable Income Systems

At the highest level of SBA commercial mortgage refinancing, success is no longer defined simply by approval, lower rates, or even portfolio growth. True mastery comes from the ability to engineer predictable, scalable, and resilient cash flow systems. This is where refinancing transitions from a financial tactic into a financial architecture—one that is intentionally designed to produce consistent income, absorb volatility, and support long-term wealth creation. In this chapter, you will learn how to engineer your cash flow using SBA refinancing, how to structure income streams that compound over time, and how to build a system that delivers predictable results regardless of market conditions.

Cash flow engineering begins with a shift in mindset. Instead of viewing cash flow as a byproduct of your assets or business operations, you begin to see it as something that can be designed and controlled. Every decision—from loan structure to reinvestment strategy—affects your cash flow. By understanding these relationships, you can intentionally create a system where income exceeds expenses in a stable and predictable way.

The first component of cash flow engineering is baseline optimization. This involves using SBA refinancing to reduce your existing debt obligations to the lowest sustainable level. By extending loan terms, securing favorable interest rates, and consolidating high-cost debt, you create a strong foundation of positive cash flow. This baseline is the starting point for all future growth, and it must be stable and reliable.

The next step is layering income streams. Instead of relying on a single source of income, you build multiple streams that contribute to your overall cash flow. This might include rental income, business revenue, and returns from investments. SBA refinancing provides the capital and flexibility needed to develop these streams, allowing you to diversify your income and reduce reliance on any one source.

Predictability is a key goal of cash flow engineering. Stable, recurring income allows you to plan more effectively and reduces financial stress. SBA loans, particularly those with fixed rates and long terms, contribute to this predictability by providing consistent payment structures. When your expenses are predictable, it becomes easier to manage and grow your income. Another important concept is margin expansion. This involves increasing the difference between your income and your expenses. SBA refinancing contributes to this by lowering your debt service, while strategic reinvestment increases your income. The wider your margin, the more resilient your financial system becomes. A strong margin provides a buffer against unexpected challenges and creates opportunities for further growth.

Velocity of money is another critical factor. This refers to how quickly you can deploy capital and generate returns. The faster you can convert savings or equity into income-producing assets, the more efficient your system becomes. SBA refinancing accelerates this process by unlocking capital and improving cash flow, allowing you to reinvest more quickly.

Another key element is reinvestment discipline. Not all income should be spent—much of it should be reinvested to generate additional returns. This creates a compounding effect, where each reinvestment increases your overall cash flow. Over time, this compounding can lead to exponential growth.

Expense control is equally important. While increasing income is a primary goal, managing expenses ensures that your gains are not eroded. This includes not only operating expenses but also debt obligations. SBA refinancing helps control expenses by providing more efficient financing structures, but ongoing management is essential to maintaining efficiency.

Stress testing your cash flow system is another critical step. By modeling different scenarios—such as decreases in income or increases in expenses—you can evaluate how your system performs under pressure. This helps you identify potential weaknesses and make adjustments before they become problems.

Another advanced concept is cash flow stacking. This involves combining multiple sources of income in a way that maximizes overall returns. For example, rental income from multiple properties can be layered with business revenue to create a larger, more stable income base. SBA refinancing supports this strategy by providing the capital needed to acquire and improve assets.

Automation and systems play a role as well. As your cash flow system grows, managing it manually becomes more complex. Implementing systems for tracking income, managing expenses, and monitoring performance ensures that your system remains efficient and scalable.

Risk mitigation remains a constant consideration. While increasing cash flow is the goal, it must be done in a way that maintains stability. This includes maintaining reserves, avoiding excessive leverage, and ensuring that your income streams are reliable.

Another important factor is alignment with your long-term goals. Your cash flow system should support your broader objectives, whether that involves financial independence, portfolio growth, or business expansion. Each decision should be evaluated based on how it contributes to these goals.

Finally, consistency is what transforms cash flow engineering into a long-term success. By consistently applying these principles and continuously refining your system, you can create a financial structure that delivers reliable and increasing income over time.

By the end of this chapter, you will understand how to design and implement a cash flow system using SBA refinancing. You will be able to optimize your baseline, layer income streams, and create a structure that supports long-term growth and stability. With the right approach, your cash flow becomes not just a result of your efforts, but a system that works for you continuously.

Real-Life Math Example: Engineering a Predictable Cash Flow System

Consider a business owner named Daniel who owns a commercial property valued at $2,200,000 with a current loan balance of $1,300,000 at 7.5%. His monthly payment is approximately $12,800. He refinances using an SBA loan at 6.5% over 25 years, reducing his payment to $8,800. This creates a monthly savings of $4,000.

Daniel uses this $4,000 to begin building his cash flow system. Over one year, he accumulates $48,000. He combines this with a $150,000 cash-out refinance, giving him $198,000 to invest in a new property.

The new property costs $700,000 and generates $7,000 in monthly rental income. With financing, his monthly payment is $4,500, leaving net cash flow of $2,500. Daniel now has an additional $2,500 in monthly income on top of his $4,000 in savings, totaling $6,500.

In the second year, Daniel reinvests this $6,500 monthly cash flow, accumulating $78,000. He uses this along with additional equity to acquire another property generating $3,000 in monthly cash flow. His total monthly income now increases to $9,500.

Over time, Daniel continues this process, reinvesting his income and leveraging his equity. After five years, he owns multiple properties generating over $20,000 in monthly cash flow. His original refinancing decision has evolved into a system that produces predictable and scalable income. Additionally, Daniel maintains a reserve fund equal to six months of expenses, ensuring that his system can withstand fluctuations in income. This adds stability and reduces risk.

This example demonstrates how SBA refinancing can be used to engineer a cash flow system. By optimizing his baseline, layering income streams, and reinvesting consistently, Daniel creates a financial structure that generates reliable income and supports long-term growth.

Chapter 14

From Refinancing to Financial Freedom — Designing Your Ultimate Wealth Blueprint

At this stage, SBA commercial mortgage refinancing is no longer just a tool—it becomes the foundation of a complete wealth-building system. The journey that begins with lowering payments and improving cash flow can ultimately lead to financial independence, where your assets generate enough income to support your lifestyle without the need for active work. This transformation does not happen by accident. It is the result of a clearly defined blueprint, executed consistently over time. In this chapter, you will learn how to connect all the strategies you have developed throughout this book into a cohesive plan that leads to long-term financial freedom.

Financial freedom begins with a clear definition of your target. You must determine how much income you need to live the life you desire. This includes not only your basic expenses but also your goals, such as travel, investments, and legacy planning. Once you have a target monthly income, you can begin to reverse-engineer your strategy, using SBA refinancing and investment principles to build toward that number. The foundation of your wealth blueprint is cash flow. Every refinancing decision should contribute to increasing your net monthly income. By consistently reducing debt payments and reinvesting the savings into income-producing assets, you create a system that generates increasing levels of cash flow over time. This process is cumulative—each improvement builds on the previous one, creating momentum that accelerates your progress.

Asset accumulation is the next critical component. Through SBA refinancing, you gain access to capital that can be used to acquire additional properties or expand your business. Each new asset adds to your income and increases your overall net worth. The key is to focus on assets that produce reliable, predictable income rather than speculative gains. This ensures that your growth is sustainable and aligned with your long-term goals.

Leverage remains a powerful tool in this process. By using borrowed capital to acquire assets, you can accelerate your growth beyond what would be possible with cash alone. However, leverage must be managed carefully. The goal is to use it as a tool for expansion without creating excessive risk. SBA programs provide a balanced approach, offering high leverage with structured, long-term repayment options. Another important aspect of your blueprint is reinvestment.

Instead of consuming all of your income, you allocate a portion toward acquiring additional assets. This reinvestment creates a compounding effect, where each new asset generates income that can be used to acquire even more assets. Over time, this compounding becomes the primary driver of your growth.

Diversification also plays a role in building a resilient wealth blueprint. By spreading your investments across different types of assets or income streams, you reduce your exposure to risk. SBA refinancing can support diversification by providing the capital needed to explore new opportunities while maintaining a stable financial structure.

Debt optimization is another key element. Not all debt is created equal. The goal is to replace inefficient, high-cost debt with structured, long-term financing that supports your cash flow. SBA refinancing allows you to transform your debt into a strategic asset, aligning it with your growth objectives.

Time is one of the most powerful forces in wealth creation. The earlier you begin implementing your blueprint, the more time you have for compounding to work in your favor. Consistency over time is more important than any single transaction. By maintaining discipline and continuing to execute your strategy, you can achieve significant results. Another critical factor is lifestyle alignment. Your financial strategy should support the life you want to live. This includes not only your income goals but also your level of involvement in your business or investments. As your income grows, you may choose to reduce your workload, transition to passive income, or pursue new opportunities.

Risk management remains essential throughout the process. Building wealth is not just about maximizing returns—it is about preserving what you have built. Maintaining reserves, managing leverage, and ensuring that your income streams are stable are all critical to long-term success.

Scaling your blueprint is what ultimately leads to financial freedom. As your system becomes more efficient, you can increase the number and size of your transactions, accelerating your growth. SBA refinancing provides the flexibility and capital needed to support this scaling process.

Another important concept is milestone tracking. Setting and achieving incremental goals helps you stay focused and measure your progress. Whether it is reaching a certain level of monthly income or acquiring a specific number of properties, these milestones provide motivation and direction.

Legacy planning is also an important consideration. Financial freedom is not just about your own success—it is about creating something that can benefit others. Whether you plan to pass on your assets to family members or contribute to your community, your blueprint should reflect your values and long-term vision.

Finally, adaptability ensures that your blueprint remains effective over time. Market conditions, personal goals, and opportunities will change, and your strategy must evolve accordingly. SBA refinancing provides the flexibility needed to adjust your approach while maintaining a strong foundation.

By the end of this chapter, you will have a complete framework for turning SBA refinancing into a pathway to financial freedom. You will understand how to define your goals, build your system, and execute your strategy in a way that creates lasting wealth and stability.

Real-Life Math Example: Building a Financial Freedom Blueprint

Consider a business owner named Sofia who determines that she needs $25,000 per month to achieve financial freedom. She begins with a commercial property valued at $2,000,000 with a loan balance of $1,200,000 at 7.5%, resulting in a monthly payment of $12,000. After refinancing with an SBA loan at 6.5% over 25 years, her payment drops to $8,200, creating a monthly savings of $3,800. Sofia reinvests this $3,800 each month. Over one year, she accumulates $45,600.

She combines this with a $150,000 cash-out refinance, giving her $195,600 to invest in a second property.

The second property generates $2,800 in monthly cash flow. Sofia's total monthly income now includes her $3,800 savings plus $2,800 from the new property, totaling $6,600. She continues this process, reinvesting her income and acquiring additional properties.

In the second year, her monthly cash flow increases to $10,000. By the third year, it reaches $15,000. By the fifth year, she surpasses her target, generating over $26,000 per month in income.

At this point, Sofia has achieved financial freedom. Her assets generate enough income to cover her expenses, allowing her to choose how she spends her time. She continues to manage her portfolio and reinvest strategically, further increasing her income and net worth.

This example demonstrates how SBA refinancing can be used as the foundation of a financial freedom blueprint. By consistently reducing expenses, reinvesting savings, and scaling her portfolio, Sofia is able to achieve her goals and create a sustainable source of income.

Chapter 15

The Complete SBA Refinancing Blueprint — From First Deal to Legacy Wealth

At this point, you have explored every layer of SBA commercial mortgage loan refinancing—from foundational concepts to advanced strategies, from risk management to scaling, and from cash flow engineering to financial freedom. This final chapter brings everything together into one unified blueprint. The purpose of this blueprint is simple yet powerful: to give you a clear, repeatable path that takes you from your first refinance all the way to building legacy-level wealth. This is where strategy becomes execution, and execution becomes transformation.

The SBA refinancing blueprint begins with awareness. You must first recognize that your current financial structure is not fixed—it can be optimized, improved, and transformed. Many business owners operate for years under inefficient debt structures simply because they are unaware of better options. The first step is to analyze your current loans, identify inefficiencies, and understand how refinancing can improve your position. This awareness is what initiates the entire process.

The second step is optimization. This is where you execute your first SBA refinance to reduce your monthly payments, improve your interest rate, and create immediate cash flow benefits. This step lays the foundation for everything that follows. The goal is not just to improve your situation slightly, but to create a meaningful shift in your financial structure that frees up capital and increases flexibility.

Once optimization is complete, the next step is stabilization. This involves ensuring that your new financial structure is sustainable and aligned with your goals. You focus on building reserves, improving your financial metrics, and creating a margin of safety. Stability is critical because it allows you to move forward with confidence, knowing that your foundation is secure.

The fourth step is expansion. With improved cash flow and access to capital, you begin to reinvest into your business or acquire additional assets. This is where the growth phase begins. Each new investment is evaluated based on its ability to generate income and contribute to your overall strategy. SBA refinancing provides the fuel for this expansion, enabling you to scale more quickly than would be possible otherwise. The fifth step is systemization. As you complete multiple transactions, you begin to develop a repeatable process. This includes standardized methods for identifying opportunities, analyzing deals, structuring loans, and reinvesting capital. Systemization is what transforms individual deals into a scalable strategy. It allows you to operate more efficiently and handle increasing levels of activity without becoming overwhelmed.

The sixth step is compounding. As your income grows and your assets increase, you begin to experience the power of compounding. Each new investment generates additional cash flow, which can be reinvested into further opportunities. Over time, this creates exponential growth. The key to compounding is consistency—continuing to apply your system and reinvest your returns.

The seventh step is optimization at scale. As your portfolio grows, you revisit your existing assets and refinance them again when beneficial. This continuous optimization ensures that your financial structure remains efficient and aligned with current market conditions. It also allows you to unlock additional equity and further accelerate your growth.

The eighth step is diversification. As your wealth increases, you expand into different types of assets or income streams. This reduces risk and creates a more resilient financial system.

SBA refinancing can support diversification by providing the capital needed to explore new opportunities while maintaining a stable foundation.

The ninth step is transition. As you approach your financial goals, you begin to shift your focus from growth to sustainability. This may involve reducing leverage, locking in long-term fixed rates, or transitioning to more passive income streams. The goal is to preserve what you have built while maintaining your desired level of income.

The tenth and final step is legacy. This is where your efforts extend beyond your own lifetime. Whether through succession planning, estate planning, or charitable contributions, your financial system becomes a tool for creating lasting impact. SBA refinancing plays a role in this stage by ensuring that your assets are structured in a way that supports continuity and long-term value.

Throughout this blueprint, discipline and consistency are essential. Each step builds on the previous one, and skipping steps or rushing the process can create challenges. By following the blueprint methodically, you create a strong foundation that supports sustainable growth.

Another important aspect is adaptability. While the blueprint provides a structured path, it must be adjusted based on your unique circumstances and changing conditions. Market dynamics, personal goals, and opportunities will evolve, and your strategy must evolve with them.

Tracking progress is also critical. By measuring your results and comparing them to your goals, you can identify areas for improvement and ensure that you remain on track. This ongoing evaluation allows you to refine your strategy and maximize your outcomes.

Mindset plays a significant role in executing this blueprint. Viewing refinancing as a strategic tool rather than a one-time event allows you to approach each decision with intention and clarity. This perspective is what enables you to build a system rather than simply completing transactions.

Finally, it is important to recognize that this blueprint is not just about financial success—it is about creating freedom, flexibility, and opportunity. By mastering SBA refinancing and applying it consistently, you can design a life that aligns with your values and goals.

By the end of this chapter, you have a complete roadmap for using SBA refinancing to build wealth, scale your portfolio, and create a lasting legacy. The strategies outlined in this book are not theoretical—they are practical tools that can be applied to real-world situations. With the right approach, discipline, and execution, you can turn these strategies into results that transform your financial future.

Real-Life Math Example: From First Refinance to Legacy Wealth

Consider an investor named Miguel who begins with a single commercial property valued at $1,500,000 and a loan balance of $1,000,000 at 7.5%. His monthly payment is approximately $9,800. He refinances using an SBA loan at 6.5% over 25 years, reducing his payment to $6,800 and creating monthly savings of $3,000.

Miguel saves this $3,000 each month, accumulating $36,000 in one year. He combines this with a $120,000 cash-out refinance, giving him $156,000 to invest in a second property. The second property generates $2,500 in monthly cash flow.

Now Miguel's total monthly improvement is $5,500. In the second year, he reinvests this income, acquiring a third property that generates $3,000 per month. His total monthly cash flow increases to $8,500.

Over the next three years, Miguel continues this process, acquiring additional properties and increasing his monthly cash flow to over $20,000. He then begins to refinance his existing properties again, reducing his debt costs and unlocking additional equity. By year seven, Miguel owns multiple properties generating $35,000 in monthly cash flow. He begins to transition his strategy, focusing on stability and long-term fixed rates. He reduces leverage slightly and builds significant reserves.

By year ten, Miguel's portfolio is valued at over $10,000,000, with total monthly cash flow exceeding $50,000. His debt is structured efficiently, and his income is stable and predictable.

At this stage, Miguel has achieved financial independence and created a system that can support future generations. His portfolio continues to generate income, and his refinancing strategy ensures that his financial structure remains optimized.

This example demonstrates how the SBA refinancing blueprint can be applied over time to create significant wealth. By starting with a single transaction and consistently applying the same principles, Miguel transforms his financial position and builds a legacy of lasting value.

Closing Thoughts

Turning Knowledge into Action and Building Your Future

You have now reached the end of this journey through SBA commercial mortgage loan refinancing, but in many ways, this is where your real journey begins. Everything you have learned throughout this series—every strategy, every concept, every example—is only as valuable as your ability to apply it. Knowledge alone does not create change. Action does. The purpose of this book, and the entire SBA Commercial Mortgage Loan Mastery Series, is to give you not just information, but a clear pathway forward. A pathway that allows you to take control of your financial structure, improve your cash flow, scale your assets, and ultimately build a life defined by freedom, flexibility, and opportunity.

One of the most important takeaways from this book is that your financial situation is not fixed. It is dynamic. It can be improved, optimized, and transformed. Many business owners and investors spend years operating under inefficient debt structures simply because they believe that is the way things have to be. This mindset limits growth and creates unnecessary financial pressure. By understanding how SBA refinancing works, you have unlocked the ability to reshape your financial foundation. You now have the tools to reduce costs, improve stability, and create opportunities that were previously out of reach.

Another key lesson is the power of intentionality. Every financial decision you make should be aligned with your goals. Whether you are looking to improve cash flow, expand your business, build a portfolio, or achieve financial independence, your refinancing strategy should support that objective. This requires clarity, planning, and discipline. It means thinking beyond the immediate transaction and considering how each decision fits into your long-term vision. When your actions are aligned with your goals, progress becomes not only possible but inevitable.

Cash flow has been a central theme throughout this book for a reason. It is the engine that drives everything else. Without strong cash flow, growth is difficult, stability is uncertain, and opportunities are limited. With strong cash flow, you gain flexibility, resilience, and the ability to act. SBA refinancing provides one of the most effective ways to improve cash flow, but it is up to you to use that improvement wisely. The way you deploy your savings and capital determines the trajectory of your financial future.

You have also seen how powerful compounding can be. Small improvements, when applied consistently over time, can lead to extraordinary results. A reduction in your monthly payment may seem modest at first, but when that savings is reinvested, it creates additional income, which can then be reinvested again. This cycle continues, building momentum with each step. Over time, this compounding effect transforms your financial position in ways that are difficult to achieve through a single transaction.

Risk management is another critical component of long-term success. Growth without stability is fragile. The strategies outlined in this book are designed not only to increase your income but also to protect it. By structuring your debt effectively, maintaining reserves, and planning for different scenarios, you create a system that can withstand challenges and continue to perform over time. This balance between growth and stability is what separates sustainable success from short-term gains.

It is also important to recognize that this process requires patience. Building wealth through SBA refinancing is not an overnight achievement. It is a long-term strategy that unfolds over years, not weeks or months. There will be periods of rapid progress and periods of slower growth. What matters is consistency. By continuing to apply the principles you have learned, even when progress seems gradual, you will move steadily toward your goals. Another powerful idea is that of control. When you understand how to structure your financing, manage your cash flow, and deploy your capital, you gain control over your financial future. You are no longer reacting to circumstances—you are shaping them. This sense of control brings confidence, and that confidence allows you to make better decisions and pursue opportunities more effectively.

As you move forward, it is important to build a system around your efforts. This includes creating processes for identifying opportunities, analyzing deals, and executing transactions. It also involves building relationships with lenders, advisors, and other professionals who can support your journey. A strong system and network can significantly enhance your ability to implement the strategies in this book.

You should also remain adaptable. The financial landscape is constantly changing, and your strategy must evolve with it. Interest rates will rise and fall, market conditions will shift, and new opportunities will emerge. By staying informed and maintaining flexibility, you can adjust your approach and continue to make progress regardless of external conditions.

Another important consideration is purpose. While financial success is a significant achievement, it is ultimately a means to an end. The true value of what you are building lies in how it enhances your life and the lives of others. Whether it is providing for your family, creating opportunities for your children, or contributing to your community, your financial system becomes a tool for achieving something greater.

As you reflect on everything you have learned, take a moment to consider where you are today and where you want to be. Define your goals clearly. Identify your next step. Then take action. The strategies in this book are not meant to be admired–they are meant to be used. Every successful journey begins with a single step, and your first step may be as simple as reviewing your current loans and exploring your refinancing options.

Momentum is built through action. Once you complete your first refinance, you will gain experience and confidence. That confidence will make the next step easier. Over time, these steps will compound, creating a system that drives continuous growth. This is how ordinary financial decisions become extraordinary results.

Remember that you do not need to have everything figured out before you begin. Progress comes from taking action, learning from experience, and refining your approach. Each step you take brings you closer to your goals and provides valuable insights that improve your strategy. The journey you are embarking on is not just about numbers—it is about transformation. It is about moving from limitation to possibility, from uncertainty to control, and from effort to efficiency. It is about creating a life where your financial system works for you rather than the other way around.

As you close this book, understand that you now have a powerful set of tools at your disposal. The knowledge you have gained has the potential to change your financial trajectory, but only if you choose to act on it. The opportunity is in front of you. The path is clear. The next move is yours.

Your future is not determined by where you are today—it is shaped by the decisions you make from this point forward.

How to Get a Personalized SBA Commercial Mortgage Review

If you found this book helpful, you may want to see how these strategies apply to your specific financial situation.

SBA commercial mortgage financing is highly customized—your business income, financial statements, credit profile, property type, industry, and long-term goals all play a role in determining what you qualify for and how your loan should be structured.

Every borrower's situation is different. Your revenue trends, business model, tax returns, debt obligations, ownership structure, and the type of commercial property you are purchasing, refinancing, or building all impact your options. The strategies and examples in this book are designed to teach you how SBA commercial mortgage loans work—but your actual loan approval, terms, and structure can only be determined by analyzing your real financial profile.

If you would like a no-obligation SBA Commercial Mortgage review, you can request one here:

Email: info@FinibiMortgage.com

A licensed mortgage broker will review your business financials, income structure, credit profile, and goals, and explain what SBA financing options may be available to you—including:

• SBA 7(a) commercial mortgage loans• SBA 504 fixed-rate commercial real estate financing• Owner-occupied property qualification strategies• Business acquisition with real estate financing• Commercial refinance and cash-out strategies• Construction and expansion loan structuring• Advanced SBA deal structuring to maximize approval

No cost. No pressure. No obligation.

Sincerely,

Joseph G. Correa

Finibi Mortgage Inc.

Licensed Mortgage Broker

About the Author

Joseph G. Correa is a licensed mortgage broker and the founder of Finibi Mortgage, a Florida-based brokerage specializing in SBA commercial mortgage loans, non-QM lending, and strategic real estate financing solutions for business owners, entrepreneurs, and investors.

With more than two decades of experience in mortgage lending, underwriting, and deal structuring, Joseph has helped thousands of clients secure financing for commercial real estate, business acquisitions, and complex transactions using both traditional and alternative lending strategies.

Unlike traditional loan officers who focus only on basic qualification, Joseph's approach emphasizes **cash flow analysis, deal structuring, and strategic financing**. He believes that business owners should not be limited by rigid lending formulas, but instead empowered by understanding how to structure deals that align with lender guidelines and maximize approval potential.

Joseph is widely recognized for his expertise in:

• SBA 7(a) and SBA 504 commercial mortgage loans• Owner-occupied commercial real estate financing• Business acquisition with real estate structuring• Commercial refinance and cash flow optimization• Construction and expansion financing• Advanced loan structuring and approval strategy

Through his education platform, Finibi Academy, Joseph has trained tens of thousands of students worldwide in mortgage strategy, real estate investing, credit optimization, and financial independence.

He created the *SBA Commercial Mortgage Loan Mastery Series* to provide a clear, step-by-step roadmap for borrowers and professionals who want to understand, qualify for, and scale commercial real estate using SBA financing.

His mission is simple:

To help business owners use strategic financing to acquire assets, build cash flow, and create long-term wealth.

When he is not structuring loans or writing, Joseph works with clients across the United States to design customized SBA financing strategies aligned with their business goals and growth plans.

The SBA Commercial Mortgage Loan Mastery Series Roadmap

The Complete Guide to Using SBA Financing to Build Commercial Real Estate and Business Wealth

The purpose of *The SBA Commercial Mortgage Loan Mastery Series* is to give business owners, investors, and mortgage professionals the exact strategies used by lenders and underwriters—translated into simple, practical steps you can apply in real life.

This series takes you from beginner to advanced mastery of how to qualify, structure, and scale commercial real estate and business financing using SBA mortgage loans.

Each book builds on the last. You are not just learning how to get approved—you are learning how to control your approvals and scale your opportunities.

Book 1 — SBA Commercial Mortgage Loan Fundamentals Understand how SBA mortgage programs work, including 7(a) and 504 loans, and how to qualify.

Book 2 — Getting Approved for an SBA Commercial Mortgage Loan Learn step-by-step strategies to meet lender requirements and secure funding.

Book 3 — Owner-Occupied Property Financing with SBA Loans Learn how to buy or refinance your business property using SBA financing.

Book 4 — Buying a Business and Real Estate with SBA Financing Acquire a business and its property in one structured transaction.

Book 5 — SBA 7(a) Mortgage Loan Strategies Master flexible loan structures for business and real estate funding.

Book 6 — SBA 504 Mortgage Loans for Commercial Real Estate Use long-term fixed-rate financing for large property acquisitions.

Book 7 — Refinancing Commercial Debt with SBA Loans Lower payments, improve cash flow, and restructure existing debt.

Book 8 — SBA Loans for Construction and Expansion Build, renovate, and scale commercial properties with structured financing.

Book 9 — SBA Loan Requirements, Rates, and Structures Understand how to compare options and choose the best loan.

Book 10 — Advanced SBA Commercial Mortgage Structuring Engineer approvals and maximize leverage using expert strategies.

This series is designed to move you from:

Understanding → Execution → Scaling → Mastery

By the end, you will not just know how to qualify—you will know how to structure, analyze, and scale deals like a professional.

Educational & Financial Disclaimer

The *SBA Commercial Mortgage Loan Mastery Series* is intended for educational and informational purposes only.

This content is designed to help readers understand SBA commercial mortgage lending, real estate financing strategies, and business acquisition concepts. It is not financial, legal, tax, or investment advice.

Joseph G. Correa and Live Stronger Faster are not acting as your personal financial advisor, attorney, accountant, or mortgage professional through this publication.

SBA loan programs, underwriting guidelines, interest rates, and lender requirements may change at any time and vary by lender.

All examples in this series are for illustration purposes only and do not guarantee approval or results.

Always consult with licensed professionals before making financial decisions.

Risk Disclosure

SBA commercial mortgage lending and real estate investing involve risk.

Business performance, income stability, interest rate changes, market conditions, and lender guidelines can all impact loan approval and financial outcomes.

Borrowing against real estate or using leverage increases both potential returns and risk.

Failure to repay a loan may result in foreclosure and loss of property.

Cash flow, rental income, appreciation, and business performance are not guaranteed.

All strategies presented in this series are educational and must be evaluated based on your individual financial situation.

You are solely responsible for your financial decisions.

www.ingramcontent.com/pod-product-compliance
Lightning Source LLC
LaVergne TN
LVHW022225200926
848481LV00006B/2131